# ROYAL CITIES
# OF THE OLD
# TESTAMENT

BY THE SAME AUTHOR

*Excavations at the Jewry Wall, Leicester*
*Beginning in Archaeology*
*Digging up Jericho*
*Jericho I and II : Tombs Excavated 1952–57*
*Archaeology in the Holy Land*
*Amorites and Jebusites*
*Jerusalem : Excavating 3000 Years of History*

PART AUTHOR OF

*Samaria–Sebasta*

# ROYAL CITIES OF THE OLD TESTAMENT

KATHLEEN KENYON

SCHOCKEN BOOKS · NEW YORK

Published in U.S.A. in 1971
by Schocken Books Inc.
67 Park Avenue, New York, N.Y. 10016

Library of Congress Catalog Card No. 79–159482

*Printed in Great Britain*

# CONTENTS

# LIST OF PLATES

# LIST OF PLANS
# AND DIAGRAMS

# CHRONOLOGY

Dates for Palestine are dependent on the Egyptian calendar, which was based on astronomical observations. These can be astronomically related to the modern calendar. With a varying degree of precision, the recorded regnal years of the Egyptian rulers can be fitted in to the astronomical calendar. There are elements of doubt, and the dates preferred by different scholars vary. For the first millennium B.C., the variation is of a few years only, but for the earlier period may be of some decades. The earliest fixed dates are about 3000 B.C.

In Palestine, the framework for dating down to about 1000 B.C. has to be provided by archaeological evidence, essentially that of pottery. Over the last seventy years, and especially over the last fifty, a relatively close and exact succession of pottery styles has been established, so that one can ascribe stages in the occupation of a town to, for instance, Early Bronze III or Late Bronze I. These periods can be given an approximate date in years either by the find of datable Egyptian (or occasionally Mesopotamian) objects in association with the typical indigenous pottery, or by events historically recorded in Egypt which can be associated with stages revealed by excavation in the history of sites. Examples of the former method are the discovery of scarabs with the name of an Egyptian ruler in a Palestinian context. Examples of the latter method are the recorded destruction of Megiddo by Thotmes III in 1480 B.C., which can be linked with a destruction of the city revealed by excavation, or of the campaign of Shishak I in Palestine in 922–921 B.C., to which is ascribed the destruction found at a number of Palestinian sites.

It is only from the time of David that the written records are sufficiently exact for an internal time scale of regnal years to be established and the first firmly fixed date is the death of Solomon. The years given for the period of the Judges and earlier are far too schematic and traditional to provide any exact evidence. The time scale of the regnal years between the establishment of the United Monarchy and the end of the Kingdom of Judah is detailed and almost exact. To be given fixed dates in modern calendar years it still needs to be linked with the Egyptian calendar, which is possible at a number of points. Owing, however, to the slightly varying interpretations possible of both the Egyptian and Israelite records, different authorities may prefer slightly different dates. The following outline chronology lists the most usually accepted dates that are relevant to this book. Where a date is exact, it is usually necessary to give it thus, 826–825 B.C., since the Israelite year ran from autumn to autumn.

| | |
|---|---|
| c. 1900 B.C. | Beginning of the Middle Bronze Age, with Canaanite city states in contact with the Middle Kingdom of Egypt. |
| Late 18th century B.C. | Egyptian Middle Kingdom disrupted by Asiatic invaders, the Hyksos. |
| c. 1560 B.C. | Beginning of the Late Bronze Age, with restoration of Egyptian influence in Palestine under the 18th Dynasty. |
| c. 1390–1360 | Period of the Amarna letters, recording the invasions of Ḥabiru warrior bands in Palestine and Syria. |
| 14th–13th century B.C. | Infiltration of Hebrew Israélite tribes into Palestine. |
| c. 1225 B.C. | The stele of Merneptah refers to 'the people Israel'. |
| c. 1196 B.C. | Rameses III's repulse of the Sea Peoples from Egypt, followed by the settlement of the Philistines on the coast of Palestine. |
| 12th–11th century B.C. | Period of the Judges and of growing struggle with the Philistines. |
| Late 11th century B.C. | Emergence of Saul as a leader of all the Israelite tribes. |
| c. 1005 B.C. | On death of Saul, David elected king of the southern tribes and about two years later, of the northern tribes, ruling from Hebron. |
| c. 966 B.C. | Death of David and accession of Solomon. |
| c. 962 B.C. | Beginning of building of the Temple at Jerusalem. |
| 926–925 B.C. | Death of Solomon. Rehoboam succeeds Solomon in Judah, but the northern tribes refuse to accept him and elect Jeroboam as King of Israel. |
| c. 878 B.C. or 886 B.C. | Omri usurps power in Israel and captures Terzah. |
| c. 872 B.C. or 880 B.C. | Omri establishes capital at Samaria. |
| 845–844 B.C. | Jehu drives out Omrid dynasty at Samaria and establishes his own. |
| c. 745 B.C. | Growth of threat to Israel and Judah from the expanding Assyrian Empire. |
| 733 B.C. | Tiglath-pileser III annexes greater part of the north of Israel. Destruction of Megiddo and Hazor. |
| 724–722 B.C. | Samaria besieged by Shalmaneser V and captured by Sargon III. End of Kingdom of Israel. |
| 701 B.C. | Lachish besieged and captured by Sennacherib. Jerusalem besieged, but saved by efforts of Hezekiah. |
| 639–638 B.C. | Succession of Josiah in Jerusalem. Some extension of power into the area of Israel. |
| 621–620 B.C. | Reform of religion carried out by Josiah. |
| 609 B.C. | Babylonian Empire succeeds Assyrian Empire as ruler in Mesopotamia. |
| 598 B.C. | Capture and destruction of Jerusalem by the Babylonians under Nebuchadnezzar. |
| 589 B.C. | Revolt of Zedekiah against Babylon. |
| 587 B.C. | Capture and final destruction of Jerusalem by Nebuchadnezzar. End of the Kingdom of Judah. |

ABOVE
*Pl. 1. Bliss and Dickie tunnels at Jerusalem, Site F.*

BELOW
*Pl. 2. Bliss and Dickie tunnel at Jerusalem.*

# 1 ❦ INTRODUCTION

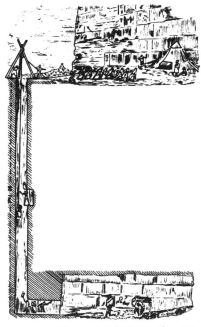

*Fig. 1. Warren's shaft at the S.E. corner of the Haram.*

The title of this book is derived from that of a lecture given in connection with the centenary celebrations of the Palestine Exploration Fund in 1965. For a hundred years the Fund had been probing into the history of Palestine. Probing is a word in fact very appropriate to the early stages of the explorations. Jerusalem was very naturally the first point of attack, and Jerusalem was probed by the incredible vertical shafts, up to 80 ft. in depth (fig. 1) through rubble that ran like water, of Warren who was the Fund's first excavator, whose work began in 1867,[1] for which the centenary is marked by the completion of the latest attack on Jerusalem. The ancient remains were also very literally probed by the next excavations of the Fund, those of F. G. Bliss and his surveyor A. C. Dickie between 1894 and 1897.[2] Their probes, though including shafts 70 ft. deep, were more in the horizontal sense, tunnels not more than 3 ft. wide and 5 ft. high, running mole-like in to pick up the lines of walls or other features for a distance of, in one case, 400 ft.[3] In our recent excavations at the southern end of the original site of Jerusalem, time and time again, having dug down anything up to 30 or 40 ft., we have encountered these mole-runs, and have marvelled how the excavators had managed to penetrate incredible distances through twisted masses of fallen stones in such constricted probes.

Today, one tends to be scornful of such probes. But one has to admit that these early excavators very literally put on the map—for they produced plans—a vast amount of information concerning ancient remains. Today it would have taken five times as long, and cost ten times as much (the multiples are figurative only), to produce the basic information. But our justification is that the information of the pioneers is only basic.

[1] *Excavations at Jerusalem 1867–70,* C. Warren.
[2] *Excavations at Jerusalem 1894–1897,* F. G. Bliss and A. C. Dickie.
[3] *Ibid.,* pp. 172 and 169.

1

They traced the lines of the walls, but they could not date them. To date a structure of any sort, one has to establish the original surface associated with it, and the date of objects, especially pottery, contained in the material inserted when the wall was built. They neither knew how to recognise the levels that were contemporary with, or earlier or later than, a wall— that is to say the stratification—nor how to assess the evidence of the associated finds. All this is the accumulated knowledge of the subsequent hundred years, drawing on the more advanced techniques of European archaeology and through them producing the local evaluation of evidence.

The probing stages in Jerusalem represent the first major steps in the exploration of Palestine. The probing stage did not outlive the 19th century. In the sponsorship of the excavations of Gezer, a site very relevant to the present theme, carried out between 1902 and 1909, the Palestine Exploration Fund sponsored a very radical approach to the problem of investigating ancient remains. Professor R. A. S. Macalister, a noted Irish archaeologist, saw that one could not produce a real history of a site by probing to find its walls. The site must be fully excavated; the interior of the city must be investigated side by side with the defences. Gezer was therefore excavated and stripped. The records, and the careful study of what was considered to be their implications, and of the finds, are a model to all subsequent generations. But what was lacking was evidence of stratification. What finds were associated with what building phases? This may sound very elementary. One building is constructed on top of another, and the evidence from the later floors is compared with that from the earlier floors, and the relative date established; in parenthesis it must be noted that at times earlier than the appearance of immediately datable objects such as coins, all this depends on the gradual accumulation of data for the chronology of, especially, pottery and of other objects commonly found. But this simplified situation seldom exists. Buildings are terraced, floors are worn away, pits are dug and, more disturbing of evidence than anything else in areas where buildings are of stone, whole wall foundations are dug up to recover the stone for subsequent use. The answer to this is observed stratigraphy, the visual evidence (recorded in drawn sections) that a surface ran to a wall, sealing the foundation trench cut when its foundations were laid; that a rubbish pit was cut into this surface at a later date; that a wall of a room was completely removed when its successor was built; *and,* most important of all, the digging methods must provide the evidence to enable one to say which objects come from the foundation trench, from the pit, from the robber trench of the wall.

These are the requirements of modern excavation methods which have been developed mainly in England, which first began to be applied in Palestine in the 1930s and were fully established there after the Second World War.

This excursus has been necessary to show why the results of the excavations at Gezer are almost worthless today. They were the result of pioneer work, but they could not cope with the terribly difficult problems of a site occupied for millennia, with the structures of each period enormously disturbing those of its predecessor.

Between the two world wars, exploration of ancient sites was very much expanded. Some of the important Biblical sites had been attacked at an earlier stage, for instance Megiddo, Samaria and Ta'anach. The major exploration of Megiddo, Beth-shan and Samaria came, however, in the inter-war period. This was a period in which very considerable steps were taken towards scientific methods of excavation. Sir Flinders Petrie in his pioneer excavations at Tell el-Hesi, as long ago as 1890, had introduced into Palestine a basic conception of stratigraphy, in which the accumulation of successive building stages was recognised and the objects were recorded in horizontal levels. These very roughly accorded with the levels of successive building stages, but the method takes no cognisance of disturbances or terraces or any other complications. It was a method which, except for the problem of terraces, could be very valuable for sites in which the buildings were of mud-brick, but was completely inapplicable to the much more complicated problems of sites where the buildings were of stone, with their infinitely more confused history in which each building was a quarry for its successor.

In this inter-war period, the Palestine Exploration Fund sponsored two more campaigns in Jerusalem, that of Professor Macalister in 1923 to 1925 and that of Mr. J. W. Crowfoot in 1927. The largest-scale excavation of the period was that of the Oriental Institute of Chicago at Megiddo. From 1931 to 1935, the Palestine Exploration Fund, in collaboration with the British School of Archaeology in Jerusalem, Harvard University and the Hebrew University, excavated at Samaria.

In Jerusalem, Megiddo and Samaria we have three of the royal cities of the Old Testament. The first category is that of the cities for which Solomon raised the levy recorded in I Kings 9. 15,[4] to which belong Jerusalem and Megiddo. To the second category belongs Samaria, the final capital of the Northern Kingdom after the break-up of the United Monarchy of David and Solomon. Of the remaining cities in the first category, reference has already been made to the excavation of Gezer. The excavation of the fourth Royal City of Solomon

[4] 'And this is the reason of the levy which King Solomon raised; for to build the house of the Lord, and his own house, and Millo and the wall of Jerusalem, and Hazor, and Megiddo, and Gezer.'

belongs to the post-war years, to the excavations of Professor Yigael Yadin between 1955 and 1958. To the second category belongs Tirzah, which preceded Samaria as the capital of the Northern Kingdom. The excavations of Père R. de Vaux, O.P., have shown that this is to be identified with Tell el Far'ah, near Nablus.

The excavations of the last hundred years, thus, have given us basic evidence concerning the original capital city of Jerusalem and the three other Royal Cities of the time of Solomon, and of Samaria, the final capital city of the Northern Kingdom and its immediate predecessor. In selecting my subject for the Centenary lecture of the Palestine Exploration Fund, I was influenced by the fact that my first introduction to Palestinian archaeology was at Samaria from 1931 to 1935, and that in 1965 I was engaged in a renewed attack on the problems of Jerusalem, begun in 1961, and culminating in 1967, just a hundred years after Warren's first excavations on behalf of the Fund.

# 2 🌿 BACKGROUND

It will surprise those to whom Palestine is known only through the Biblical story that it was only for a very brief span that there were any Royal Cities, for, down to the time in 1948 when the eastern part of the country was incorporated in the Hashemite Kingdom of Jordan, in the whole of Palestinian history there was no kingdom of Palestine except for about four hundred years from the time of David down to the Babylonian destruction in 586 B.C., for about thirty years under Herod the Great at the end of the 1st century B.C., and for a mere four years under his grandson Herod Agrippa in the middle of the 1st century A.D. For the last two thousand five hundred years, Palestine has, except for the Herodian interlude, been ruled by great empires based on adjoining countries. Down to the beginning of the 1st millennium B.C., it was a place of city states, independent of each other and, to judge from the attention lavished on the defences, often warring among themselves. In the background for much of the time there was an imperial power, usually Egypt, exercising a certain amount of control, for though Palestine was not a rich country, and not worthy of conquest on its own account, it was important as a route between Egypt and the north and east. In the struggle for power between Egypt and Syria or the successive rulers of Mesopotamia, it was important to control the route up to the coast, which turned inland near Megiddo via the Plain of Esdraelon, and crossed the Jordan on the road to Damascus. In times of peace, the route was equally important for trade.

Whenever Egypt was strong, therefore, she kept a firm hand on the important towns. It is probable that in most cases this was done simply by assuring the client status of the ruler by levying tribute rather than by direct rule. Just occasionally there is evidence of an Egyptian governor or at least envoy, for instance a statue of the time of Rameses VI, in the mid 12th century B.C., at Megiddo,[1] or in the strongly Egyptianising temple fittings at Beth-shan rather earlier,[2] but these are the exception and not the rule. A good picture of the normal state of affairs is given by the Amarna letters, c. 1390–1360 B.C.[3] These were written at a time when, after a long period of Egyptian strength in Syria, from the time of Thotmes I (1525–1512 B.C.) and especially from that of Thotmes III (1504–1450 B.C.), a period of decline set in under Akenaten (1379–1362 B.C.). Western Asia was at that time in a state of turmoil caused by the raids of the Ḥabiru, warrior bands recruited probably from the desert fringes, with whom the Hebrews are certainly connected, though it is not generally held that these movements are identical with those that brought the main body of the Israelites into Palestine. The raiders were a menace to all settled life, and the rulers of the Palestinian towns had to deal with the threat. Some apparently came to terms with them, but many rulers sent urgent letters to Egypt asking for help. The names of the rulers are native, Semitic or Ḥurrian, but there is no doubt that they write to Pharaoh as vassals. In the preceding period of Egyptian power, they had accepted Egyptian suzerainty, but now for a period this was passing into eclipse.

These city states take their origin in the Early Bronze Age. As we know from the evidence of Jericho, the first steps towards urban development occur at least as early as anywhere else, in the 8th millennium B.C. For two thousand years a Neolithic town flourished at Jericho, at a time when there were few competitors in the whole of western Asia, the cradle of civilisation. But towards 5000 B.C., town life dies out, for reasons we do not yet know. It was not until c. 3000 B.C. that full urban development began again, as it did in Mesopotamia and Egypt. But while in these two areas from amongst the growing towns leaders emerged to establish overlordship and imperial rule, no such further step forward took place in Palestine, and the pattern of city states grew up that was to be characteristic of most of the next two thousand years.

Between the urban organisation of the Early Bronze Age and that of the period of the entry of the Israelites, there is an interlude, c. 2300–1900 B.C., which introduced the Amorites into Palestine, a people shown both by the literary records and by the archaeological evidence to be essentially nomads and pastoralists, not town dwellers.[4] Soon after the re-establishment of settled rule in Egypt with the growth of the Middle Kingdom, a new urban civilisation appears in Palestine, which

[1] *M II*, pp. 135–8.
[2] *Beth-shan, Four Temples.*
[3] For the most recent treatment, see *C.A.H.* Revised edition, Vol. II, ch. XX.
[4] *C.A.H.* Revised edition, Vol. I, ch. XXI, *Amorites and Canaanites.*

can be called Canaanite, and which probably developed on the Syrian coast in the neighbourhood of Byblos.[5]

In this Middle Bronze Age of Palestine, the towns of the Early Bronze Age were largely re-occupied and re-fortified, and the culture introduced then, very close to that of the Canaanite towns of the Syrian coast, was essentially uninterrupted down to the 12th–11th centuries B.C. Politically there were some changes. In the 18th century B.C. the Hyksos, warrior bands of diverse origin, established a warrior aristocracy. Evidence of this is found in the appearance of a new type of fortification, in which great earth ramparts strengthened the actual town wall,[6] and on the side of written records evidence that by the time of the Amarna letters (c. 1390–1360 B.C.) many of the rulers bore non-Semitic names.[7] But the archaeological evidence is quite clear that the appearance of this alien warrior aristocracy did not affect the basic culture. The people who re-established the towns of Palestine c. 1900 B.C. were the inhabitants of the towns at the time of the entry of the Israelites. Our basic key for this assessment is the pottery and other common domestic objects. In this ordinary domestic equipment there is no break from c. 1900 until at least 1200 B.C. The appearance of classes of imported pottery is useful chronologically, as when the restoration of imperial power in Egypt at the beginning of the 18th Dynasty (1570 B.C.) provided peace in the eastern Mediterranean, with the result of a flood of Cypriot imports into Palestine, or when Mycenean imports begin to appear early in the 14th century B.C. But the basic indigenous pottery forms continue in an uninterrupted development and the other material evidence of indigenous culture is likewise continuous. For some seven hundred years or more, Palestine had had an unbroken Canaanite culture, with a political organization of city states, controlled to an extent which varied from time to time by Egypt.

The entry of the Israelites into Palestine was not the simple, one-stream affair that the Biblical account would suggest. To understand this, one has to understand how the Biblical record has come down to us. The final result bears the mark of a whole succession of editors, who endeavoured to combine the material available to them into one coherent record describing a continuous succession of events. This available material consisted basically of tribal records. The tribal make-up of the Israelites is very evident from the Biblical record, though even this is complicated by the appearance and disappearance of tribes. The records of those tribes were certainly oral, for though written documents are known from the Semitic area in profusion from Syria by the 15th century B.C.,

[5] *Amorites and Canaanites,* pp. 51–59.
[6] *Amorites and Canaanites,* pp. 65–73.
[7] *C.A.H.* Revised edition, Vol. II, ch. XX. (Published as Fascicle 51, p. 13.)

there is no evidence at all that the invading, semi-nomadic, Israelites were literate until much later. Critical analysis of the traditions that lie behind the first written documents incorporated in the Bible accounts[8] shows that there was no single entry of the Israelites, but rather a diverse and sporadic infiltration of groups which ultimately coalesced, and amongst whom the story of the Exodus, which belonged to the history of one group, assumed, by the time the editors attacked the task of combining all the records into one history, an overwhelming importance owing to the evidence it gave of the favour of Yahweh towards the tribes of Israel.

The archaeological evidence emphatically supports this critical analysis of the literary evidence. Archaeologically, at no one point in the history of any site can one say that the Israelites appear. The evidence at Jericho suggests a destruction and abandonment in the last quarter of the 14th century B.C.; the evidence at Hazor suggests a destruction and abandonment in the first quarter of the 13th century B.C.; at Tell Beit Mirsim and Tell Duweir there is a destruction in the second half of the 13th century B.C. But none of these destructions was certainly the work of the Israelites, and in the case of the last two, in the south and near the coast, there are other candidates as the authors of the destructions, possibly the Egyptians, possibly the Philistines, or Peoples of the Sea, who appear on the coast at the end of the thirteenth century B.C. Moreover, in those sites such as Tell Beit Mirsim at which occupation continues after the destruction, there is no immediate change of culture, on the evidence of the material remains, that would enable one to say that a new people had occupied the site.

The basic fact is that the Israelites did not bring with them a material culture. They were semi-nomads, entering the Promised Land from the desert fringes, only lightly equipped with the type of objects that can survive to us as material evidence. They infiltrated over a period that may have begun in the 14th century, and culminated at the end of the 13th century, and only gradually took possession of villages and towns. Lacking themselves a material culture, they took over that of the inhabitants of the land, that material culture of the Canaanites which had developed since c. 1900 B.C. This is shown both by the fact that there is no break in the tradition of pottery and other domestic articles until well after the date of the Israelite infiltration, and by the fact that throughout the period of the written history of the Israelite kingdoms the cult influence of Canaanite religion keeps on reappearing; the infiltrating Israelites could never completely suppress the Canaanite population that they absorbed.

The formative period of Israel as a political entity is that of

[8] For an exhaustive study of the evidence, see *Joseph to Joshua*, Lecture II.

the Judges. This is an excellent illustration of the city-state organisation into which the Israelites penetrated. The Book of Judges records that a particular leader 'judged Israel' for a period of years—ten, twenty, thirty and so on. But there is no direct succession in the list of judges. They come from different tribes, geographically widely separated. Some are Benjaminites, some are Gileadites, some belong to the tribe of Manasseh, some come from Bethlehem. They are tribal leaders, recorded in the tribal records for their successes against enemies, but in no true sense leaders of Israel. They obtain prominence because of threats, in Biblical terms, oppressions, from surrounding groups. The principal town of each tribal group was the equivalent of the central town of the city states of the Canaanites. The tribes were bound together by their common worship of Yahweh, but by no means always did they respond to calls to present a united front against enemies and, like their Canaanite predecessors, they could wage bitter war amongst themselves; a dramatic record of such warfare is contained in Judges 20, describing how the Benjaminites were almost exterminated by the northern tribes of Israel.

It was in fact the threats of enemies that created a united Israel, ruled by a king. The threats which resulted in the emergence of the various judges came mostly from adjacent kingdoms, none of them of more than local importance—from Moab, Ammon, Amalek, Midian—and the threats were temporary. But in several instances the Philistines on the west were associated in attacks with the states to the east, and it was the ultimate danger from the Philistines that brought a kingdom of Israel into being.

The Philistines are a people familiar from the Biblical story, particularly from that of Samson and of the wars of Saul. Their five cities were Gaza, Ascalon, Gath, Ashdod and Ekron (Samuel 6, 17). Historically they can be associated with the invasions of the Peoples of the Sea, which had a far-ranging effect on western Asia, and which were finally driven back from Egypt by Rameses III, for the *Pulesti* constituted one of the groups involved in this massive and aggressive folk movement. Like so many of these mass movements of antiquity, for instance those of the Hyksos and Ḥabiru, our available evidence as to their origins is imprecise. Present opinion suggests that there was an Aegean element and an Anatolian element. Historically, it is clear that when the invaders were repulsed from Egypt, some settled down on the Palestine coast, where their five cities are to be identified. Archaeologically they emerge still in a rather shadowy manner, for none of their principal cities has yet been fully excavated. The one key to their arrival at present seems to be a distinctive pottery. This pottery has a basically Aegean appearance, belonging to the general group of Late Helladic III B, especially rather heavy crater-like bowls with loop handles tilted upwards. The vessels are quite un-Palestinian both in shape and decoration. Nevertheless, the decoration does not fit tidily into the categories of any of the recognised Aegean groups, from Cyprus, from Rhodes, from Crete and so on.[9] The relationship is collateral and the ancestry mixed. It has been suggested that some of the decorative elements have an Egyptian link[10] and certainly Egypt employed Aegean mercenaries in the 13th century B.C., and the link may have come in this manner. It would be reasonable to explain the pottery as made by people who had come from an area in which pottery of this type was in use, not as direct copies but to their own ideas. The important point is that it is found in just those areas, basically along the coast with some penetration inland, in which the Philistines were established, and not in the rest of Palestine.

The original area occupied by the Philistines was on the coastal plain, where they established themselves early in the 12th century B.C.; this establishment was at the expense of the Canaanite city states, for the Israelites had not penetrated that far west. The power of the Philistines grew steadily, based on a feudal aristocracy led by the 'princes' who ruled the five main towns, and their expansionist ambitions grew with their power. Towards the end of the 11th century the whole area occupied by the Israelite tribes was threatened. The threat was so great that at last all the tribes combined to oppose it, and the Ark was brought from Shiloh as a symbol that the only uniting force, the rule of Yahweh, was involved. It was the defeat of the Israelites and the capture of the Ark that brought Saul to power, thus constituting the first step in the creation of a monarchy.

Saul's call to power was, according to the Bible,[11] inspired by his anointing by Samuel, the 'man of God'. This emergence was not unlike that of the early Judges, but it is clear that the impact of the Philistine advance was such that he could call upon all the tribes. With this support he achieved a brilliant victory over the Canaanites, who had taken advantage of the defeat of the Israelites west of the Jordan to attack the tribes east of the Jordan. This victory assured Saul's position as leader, and as a result 'the whole people' 'made Saul king before Yahweh'[12] at a general assemblage at Gilgal in the Jordan valley near Jericho, where they could meet outside the area of direct Philistine control. This constituted a major step in creating a unity out of the tribes of Israel.

Saul's emergence as a leader of the whole of Israel was

*Fig. 2. Map of Palestine.*

[9] Pendlebury, *The Relationship between Philistine and Mycenaean Pottery.*
[10] Amiran, *Philistine Civilisation in the Light of Archaeological Finds in Palestine and Egypt.*
[11] I Samuel 9. 1 to 10. 16.
[12] I Samuel 11. 15.

# The United Monarchy

**ISRAEL, JUDAH**    Hebrew kingdoms

**SYRIA, etc.**    Non-Israelite peoples

★    Places fortified by Solomon

0    10    20 Miles
0    10    20 Kilometres

V   X   Sidon   Y   ZOBAH

*THE*

*GREAT*

*SEA*

Tyre

Abel-beth-maacah   Dan   Beth-rehob

BETH-REHOB   SYRIA (ARAM)

Damascus

Mt. Lebanon   Mt. Hermon

MAACAH   BASHAN   ARGOB

Hazor ★   GESHUR

Merom

Acco

Cabul

Sea of Chinnereth

Helam

Dor   R. Kishon   HAVVOTH-JAIR

Jokneam / Jokmeam   Lo-debar

Megiddo ★   Jezreel   V. of Jezreel   Rogelim   Tob

Taanach   Mt. Gilboa   Beth-shean   Ramoth-gilead

*ISRAEL*

Arubboth   Abel-meholah

Hepher   Jabesh-gilead

Socoh   Thebez   Zarethan

Mt. Ebal   Shechem   Succoth   Mahanaim

Pirathon   Mt. Gerizim   R. Jabbok

Plain of Sharon

Joppa   Gath-rimmon   GILEAD

Zoredah   Shiloh   Jazer

Baal-hazor   AMMON

Beth-hanan   Ephraim   Rabbah (Rabbath-ammon)

Lower Beth-horon ★   Bethel   Beeroth

Gezer ★   Shaalbim   Upper Beth-horon   Gibeon   Geba   Gilgal

Baalath ★   Elon   Gibeah   Anathoth   Jericho   Heshbon

Ekron   Makaz   Kiriath-jearim   High Place ★ Jerusalem

Ashdod   Sorek   Beth-shemesh

Libnah   Bethlehem   Medeba

Ashkelon   Netophah

Gath   Adullam   Tekoa

*PHILISTINES*

Giloh

Gaza   Debir   Hebron

Gerar   Carmel   Dibon   Aroer

Ziklag   R. Arnon

Kabzeel

Brook Besor   Beer-sheba

Valley of Salt   Kir-haresheth

*The Negeb*

*AMALEK*

Tamar   Brook Zered

*EDOM*

The Lowland (Shephelah) of Judah

Wilderness of Judah   Salt Sea (Sea of the Arabah)

The River Jordan   The Arabah

R. Nahaliel

MOAB

© Oxford University Press

however a presage of what was to come rather than the start of an era. He had a short period of success in driving out the Philistine garrisons. But there are hints in the Biblical record that the tribes were not yet ready to accept a secular monarchy, and the Philistines were certainly not prepared to give up their ambitions to rule the whole country down to the Jordan. It was probably within a year of Saul's assumption of the leadership that the full might of the Philistines was assembled against the Israelites, and with an advance up the coastal plain and east through the Plain of Esdraelon, they were able to confront the levies from central Palestine and separate them from the tribes of the north and east. The defeat and death of Saul and Jonathan in the battle of Mount Gilboa are described in one of the more dramatic passages in the Old Testament.

The monarchy of Saul was of short duration, but it led the way to the creation of the monarchy of David. The early story of David is one of opportunism and ambition, which is forgotten in a national hero, but one which history cannot ignore. But here we are concerned only with his emergence as a leader who created a monarchy and the conditions for the Royal Cities for which the archaeological evidence is to be described. David achieved a position of prominence first as a favourite of Saul, as his armour-bearer. Rightly or wrongly, Saul became jealous of him, and he had to flee the court. He then joined himself to the Philistines, and his reputation as a warrior secured for him a feudal fief under Achish of Gath. From this appointment he built up his position with great political astuteness. The southern tribes of Judah called him to be their leader, and he set up his capital at Hebron. His success against the Philistines whom for a short time he had served led the northern tribes of Israel likewise to name him as king. The rule of a single man over all the tribes of Israel was established, but there was not yet a united monarchy. David ruled on the basis of separate mandates from the southern and northern tribes, and between his two realms was the physical obstacle of Jerusalem. The acquisition of Jerusalem was to create the first Royal City of the Old Testament, and the city was to be the keystone of the United Monarchy of David and Solomon.

# 3 ❧ THE SITE
# OF JERUSALEM

The importance of Jerusalem can be understood only in terms of its geographical position. In size and wealth it was in origin quite insignificant in comparison with the great cities of the plains; by the time of Solomon it had become wealthy, but it did not become a large city until Herodian times.

The physical configuration of Palestine[1] has throughout prehistory and history exercised strict control over human occupation and routes of communication. The length from north to south of Palestine at the time of the British Mandate, which is roughly equivalent to historic Palestine, is approximately 240 miles. Its width from the coast to the river Jordan averages only about 48 miles. Within this narrow strip, there are great extremes in height, in climate, in soil, in vegetation. From the Mediterranean to Jerusalem it is in a direct line 36 miles, but in these 36 miles you rise from sea level to 2,500 ft. Continuing in the same straight line you reach the Dead Sea in 17 miles, at 1,290 ft. below sea level. To the east again, a height of c. 2,500 ft. on the edge of the Transjordanian plateau is reached in a distance of about 14 miles. In effect a plateau divided from the sea by a coastal plain, narrow in the north, widening to the south, is cut into by a great trough, down which runs the river Jordan into the Dead Sea, and continuing beyond the Dead Sea as the Wadi ʿArabah and the Gulf of ʿAqaba. This trough was created by a great cataclysm which dropped, for several thousand feet, a whole strip of the earth's

[1] Fig. 2.

13

surface over a length stretching from Syria in the north to the great lakes of East Africa in the south, a cataclysm that took place in times that are recent geologically but which long precede the appearance of man.

The initial cataclysm was torturing enough to the face of the land, but its effects on the land in which men were eventually to live were greatly increased by the modifications carried out by natural causes throughout the succeeding millennia. Into the cliffs left on either side of the Jordan valley and into the seaward side of the original plateau, channels to carry off rain water have cut back in a fantastic way. Today, from shallow beginnings on either side of the plateau, such a channel, known as a *wadi*[2] or dry river bed, will deepen within a few hundred yards to a deep gash with sides at an angle of 30° or more.

These wadis have therefore eaten back into the plateau strip left between the coastal plain and the Jordan valley to create the narrow spine with spreading ribs that the physical map shows. Passage along the flanks of the ridge in a north–south direction, up and down the sides of the successive wadis, is unbelievably laborious. Rapid and large-scale communication in a north–south direction is limited to the coastal plain, to the crest of the hill country and to the Jordan valley, and to the east of the Jordan along the comparatively narrow fertile plateau area before the waterless Arabian desert begins. East–west communication is channelled into those great wadis, into which the lesser ones converge, which provide convenient access to the hills. It is in connection with the north–south route along the hill crest and related cross-valleys that the importance of the position of Jerusalem lies.

The crest of the hill country of Palestine is relatively broad to the north, while to the south the height of the ridges diminishes and the physical features become less dominating and restricting. It is in the central section that geography is most constricting, and this is where Jerusalem is situated. On either side of the Old City of Jerusalem are the first beginnings of wadis that merge and deepen rapidly to form the Wadi en-Nar running down into the Dead Sea. Only half a mile to the north-west is the head of a wadi running west into the Mediterranean. Through this narrow gap the north–south route had to pass. This gap was controlled by Jerusalem. Moreover, at this point there was a convergence of good valley routes down to the east and west, and Jerusalem was thus at a crossroads which was important throughout history.

It was this north–south route on the crest that was of importance to the Israelites during the stage of their entry into

[2] This Arabic word is treated henceforth as an Anglicised loan word.

Palestine. The coastal route was never within their power; in the 13th century B.C. the Canaanite cities there were controlled by Egypt, and in the 12th century it fell under the power of the Philistines. The Jordan valley route was of limited use, for it provided no effective contact with the south since the Dead Sea stretches from side to side of the valley with cliffs going right down to the shores. Though some of the Israelite tribes settled east of the Jordan, the greater part of the eastern plateau and the route along it were in the alien hands of Ammon, Moab and Edom. Only the route along the crest of the western hills linked the areas into which the Israelites were infiltrating.

It is now usually held that the movement of the Israelites into Palestine was a complex and gradual process. There is general agreement among scholars that there were two main groups, the tribes that were ultimately to form the kingdom of Judah coming in from the south, and those that were to form the kingdom of Israel coming in from the north-east. The tribal records of these main groups, each in itself made up of many strands, were combined by later compilers into a single epic, thus building up a story of simultaneous invasion by the whole twelve tribes and a rapid conquest of the whole country. Textual criticism has been able to unravel the strands to a certain extent, though there are still many debatable points.

The resistance of Jerusalem to the invaders appears early in the record as it has reached us, for the king of Jerusalem was one of the kings of the Amorites who fought against Joshua and was defeated by him at Gibeon.[3] The capture of Jerusalem is claimed at one point.[4] But if it was captured, it was soon lost again, for in a passage[5] which must record a stage at which the settlement of the tribes was taking shape the territory of the tribe of Judah is given as including the area of Jerusalem, but it is stated: 'And as for the Jebusites, the inhabitants of Jerusalem, the children of Judah could not drive them out: but the Jebusites dwell with the children of Judah at Jerusalem unto this day.'[6]

This successful opposition of the Jebusites was to have an effect on the history of the Israelite tribes that lasted to the end of historic Judaism in Palestine. Though the tribes entered the country as separate groups and over a period of time, with the major division between north and south referred to above, there was a feeling of racial community between them. In the incident already quoted above of the savage revenge of the northern tribes against Benjamin, the northern tribes were sufficiently tender towards those linked to them by race and religion to make provision that the few survivors should

[3] Joshua 10. 1–11.
[4] Judges 1. 8.
[5] Joshua 15.
[6] Joshua 15. 63. In Judges 1. 21, the children of Benjamin take the place of the children of Judah.

secure wives to carry on their families. But the barrier of
Jerusalem crystallised the separateness induced by entry by
different routes, at different times and into a different kind
of country. As a result, the southern group and the northern
group never amalgamated. Both asked David to be their king,
and David's capture of Jerusalem enabled him and his successor Solomon to rule all the tribes as a single kingdom. In
this, the fact that Jerusalem had belonged neither to the
southern nor the northern tribes, but was David's conquest
from the Jebusites, was an actual advantage. It was David's
own town, from which both north and south could be ruled.
But when the inspiration and genius of David and Solomon
were removed, the separatist influence of north and south
re-asserted themselves, and the United Monarchy fell apart
with the old divisions of north and south, the kingdoms of
Israel and Judah.

The major physical conformation of Palestine thus ensured
the importance of Jerusalem. Physical features also dictated
the details of the actual site, and this is the necessary background to the historical and archaeological evidence with

*Pl. 3. Air view of Jerusalem.*

*Pl. 4. Air view of Jerusalem.*

[7] For the evidence of the Hadrianic origin of the Old City, see *P.E.Q.* 1967.

[8] The term 'Old City' is used here and hereafter in the sense of the city enclosed by medieval walls which is the core of all subsequent developments, though in archaeological terms it is, as will be seen, of relatively modern origin.

which the rest of the section on Jerusalem will be concerned. Today, Jerusalem is a wide-spreading city, mainly developed by the two successor powers to the British Mandate, Israeli Jerusalem spreading widely on the west, Arab Jerusalem spreading to the north towards Ramullah. The core is the Old City, venerable today with an origin in the Aelia Capitolina of Hadrian in A.D. 135,[7] but the latest of the cities of ancient Jerusalem.

This Old City[8] of Jerusalem is an irregular quadrangular area which from the air (pls. 3 and 4) looks like a plateau, bounded to the east and west by steep valleys. This illusion of a plateau does not survive a visit to the site, for from the west to the east all streets slope markedly down, and then rise again to the present Haram esh-Sherif, the site of Solomon's Temple. This slope within the Old City is the visual evidence today of the third of the valleys that created the sites of the successive cities of Jerusalem.

The site of Jerusalem is based on spurs on the east side of the central crest. The visible valleys that define the site have an initial north–south direction, for the basic north–south

*Pl. 5. View down the Kedron valley.*

*Pl. 6. The Kedron valley from the north-east.*

direction of the central crest from which they spring has here taken a curve to the west. On the east is the Kedron valley (fig. 3, pls. 5 and 6). The origins of this valley are in a more gentle depression that curves round from the north-west, but its rapid accentuation along the eastern flanks of the Old City (pl. 6) develops the defensive potential of the site. The western limit of the Old City is marked by an equally pronounced feature, the Hinnom valley (pl. 7). The name has an evil reputation, for it is the Biblical Gehenna, unclean, for unclean refuse was, in that period, burnt here, and over it in those days hung an evil-smelling cloud of smoke. In origin, it was a physical feature like the Kedron. The original course of the Hinnom bounds the west side of the Old City. It continues south from the south-west corner of the Old City, and then turns east to join the Kedron (pl. 8).

*Pl. 7. The Hinnom valley from the east.*

These two valleys, the Kedron and the Hinnom, are the obvious physical features bounding the Old City today. They defended the site, flanking the north–south route along the crest of the hill country, that gave Jerusalem its political importance. The Jerusalem of Herod Agrippa in the 1st century A.D. covered this whole area between the Kedron and the Hinnom. This was, however, the last stage in the development of historic Jerusalem, and in the earlier stages, a central valley, to which reference has already been made, was of equal importance. This central valley was still recognised by the Jewish historian Flavius Josephus in the 1st century A.D. He calls it the Tyropoeon; the interpretation of this name as the valley of the cheese-makers is by no means certain. The valley has its origin from the main ridge near the present Damascus Gate, and its course to the south is followed by one of the main streets from the Damascus Gate, down to which the streets from the west have a marked slope. South of the walls of the Old City, the contours of the valley become apparent, but excavation has shown that 50 ft. of debris have accumulated above its base. Its convergence with the Kedron comes at a distance of 900 m. south of the walls of the Old City.

*Pl. 8. Junction of Kedron and Hinnom valleys from the south.*

The Old City of Jerusalem thus straddles the northern end of two ridges, both flanked by steep valleys. To the north these ridges merge into the main crest; here alone there is no natural defensive feature, and through the ages the north wall of Jerusalem has varied considerably. It has been the task of archaeology to establish its position, and it has also been the task of archaeology to relate the site of earliest Jerusalem to that of the Old City and to the natural features.

When the first excavators of the Palestine Exploration Fund started at Jerusalem a hundred years ago, the natural point of attack was the Old City, for that was the only Jerusalem known at that time. At an early date, however, Warren found that there was a wall running south from the south-east corner of the Haram (the Temple platform). Its line followed the crest of the Kedron valley, and in pl. 9 is indicated by the road and the line of houses that continue the line of the road. The exploration of this area south of the Old City was taken up again by Bliss and Dickie,[9] and between 1894 and 1897 they traced a continuous line from the south-west corner of the Old City round the crest of the Hinnom to its junction with the Kedron, and then north-east along the Kedron and across the mouth of the Tyropoeon to join the line following the crest of the Kedron, first found by Warren. The plan thus established is reproduced in fig. 3.

These walls therefore enclose the whole of the two ridges, and give a plan of Jerusalem limited by the Kedron and the Hinnom. Until the new excavations started in 1961 it was usually accepted that this represented Jerusalem of the period of the Jewish monarchy, with a north wall in approximately the position of the broken line that has been added to the Bliss and Dickie plan. It was, however, accepted that the earliest Jerusalem was likely to have been smaller and was likely to have been on the eastern ridge. The main point of disagreement was the date at which expansion to the western ridge took place, one view being that it was the work of Solomon,[10] another that it dates from the mid 9th century B.C.[11] and so on.

The view that original Jerusalem was on the eastern ridge did in itself require powerful advocacy, for Josephus, writing in the 1st century A.D., described the western hill as Mount Zion, and thus implied that he considered that it was here that the City of David was situated. The western ridge is in fact superficially a much more attractive site. It is higher, and at its north end overtops the original town on the eastern ridge by some 240 ft. It is much wider, and its contours much more suitable for occupation. It is open to the cool western breezes. The ancient history of Jerusalem must have been so far forgotten by the time of Josephus that these advantages

[9] B. and D.
[10] B. and D., p. 290; Simons, p. 226 ff.
[11] Vincent, J. de l'A.T., Pts. II and III, p. 639.

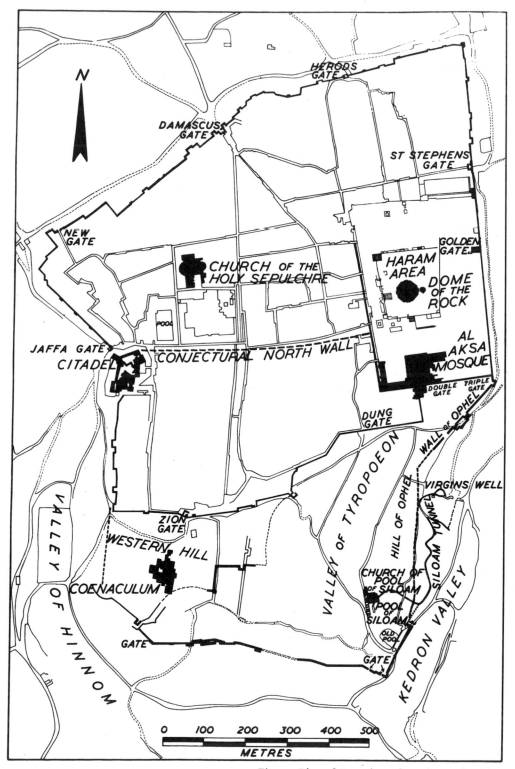

*Fig. 3. Plan of Jerusalem after Bliss and Dickie.*

were taken to indicate that here must have been the first city.

The advantage of the eastern ridge that far outweighed any other was water-supply. All towns and villages in Palestine had to be situated near a perennial water-supply until a comparatively late date, for it was not until about the beginning of the 1st millennium B.C. that the invention of lime mortar meant that it was possible to store the winter's rains round the year in cisterns. There is no perennial source of water near the western ridge. In the Kedron valley there are two springs, the Spring Gihon (the modern Virgin's Fountain or 'Ain Umm ed-Daraj) and Bir 'Ayub. The latter is south of the junction of the Hinnom with the Kedron, and therefore beyond the defensible area. It was the position of the Spring Gihon that controlled the site of Jerusalem (pl. 9) and made the eastern ridge the inevitable site of the first city.

*Pl. 9. The east slope of the eastern ridge of Jerusalem, with the site of the Spring Gihon beneath the house to the left of the boy in the foreground*

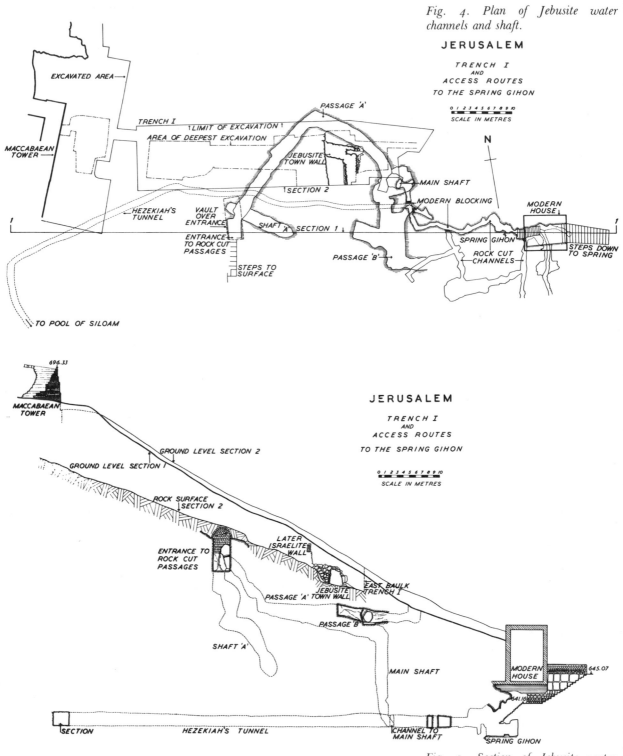

Fig. 4. Plan of Jebusite water channels and shaft.

**JERUSALEM**

TRENCH I
AND
ACCESS ROUTES
TO THE SPRING GIHON

0 1 2 3 4 5 6 7 8 9 10
SCALE IN METRES

N

EXCAVATED AREA →

TRENCH I  │LIMIT OF EXCAVATION│  PASSAGE 'A'

AREA OF DEEPEST EXCAVATION

JEBUSITE
TOWN WALL

MACCABAEAN
TOWER →

SECTION 2

MAIN SHAFT

MODERN BLOCKING

MODERN
HOUSE

HEZEKIAH'S
TUNNEL

VAULT
OVER
ENTRANCE

SHAFT 'A' SECTION 1

SPRING GIHON

STEPS DOWN
TO SPRING

ENTRANCE
TO ROCK CUT
PASSAGES

ROCK CUT
CHANNELS

PASSAGE 'B'

STEPS TO
SURFACE

I                                                                    I

TO POOL OF SILOAM

696.33

MACCABAEAN
TOWER

**JERUSALEM**

TRENCH I
AND
ACCESS ROUTES
TO THE SPRING GIHON

0 1 2 3 4 5 6 7 8 9 10
SCALE IN METRES

GROUND LEVEL SECTION 2

GROUND LEVEL SECTION 1

ROCK SURFACE
SECTION 2

ENTRANCE TO
ROCK CUT
PASSAGES

LATER
ISRAELITE
WALL

EAST BAULK
TRENCH I

PASSAGE 'A' TOWN WALL

JEBUSITE
TOWN WALL

PASSAGE B

SHAFT 'A'

MAIN SHAFT

MODERN
HOUSE

645.07

641.16

SECTION

HEZEKIAH'S TUNNEL

CHANNEL TO
MAIN SHAFT

SPRING GIHON

Fig. 5. Section of Jebusite water channels and shaft.

# 4 ✤ JERUSALEM OF THE JEBUSITES AND OF DAVID

There is no literary evidence that has any bearing on the site of Jerusalem earlier than the brief and elliptical mention in II Samuel 5. 6–9 of David's attack on the Jebusite stronghold, perhaps c. 996 B.C. The confidence of the Jebusites in the strength of their defence is shown by their jeers that it could be defended by the blind and the lame. David's reply was to offer that whosoever would get up the water channel and smite the blind and the lame, he should be captain of his host. This feat was apparently accomplished by Joab.

The implications are that there was a route to the spring from within the walls which was penetrated by Joab, who thus took the defenders by surprise from the rear, and enabled the attacking force to break in. Access to a spring in a valley outside the city site is a commonplace in Palestinian towns. The most famous are at Megiddo, Gibeon and Gezer. The skeleton of knowledge concerning tunnels connected with the Spring Gihon in the Kedron valley came from Warren's discoveries in 1867.[1] The interrelation of the various tunnels and shafts was made much more clear by Père Vincent in his study of the clearances of the 1911 excavations.[2] The earliest component was a combination of rock-cut passage and shaft, shown on figs. 4 and 5. The approach to the spring was begun at a point on the slope of the hill 43 m. west from the spring and 30 m. higher. The first attempt was apparently to sink a shaft vertically from that point, the foot of which would have been linked by a tunnel with the spring, on the model of the Megiddo water system.[3] The shaft ran into difficulties from very hard rock strata, and was abandoned after a depth of 23 m. was reached. The second and successful attack on the

[1] Warren, *R.J.*, pp. 239–42.
[2] Vincent, *J.s.T.*
[3] See pp. 101–3.

*Pl. 10. Macalister's so-called 'Tower of David', in reality Maccabean.*

problem was to run a sloping rock-cut passage to a point 25 m. further to the north-east. To lessen the steepness of the slope, the passage follows a zig-zag line, just as a surface path would in such circumstances, and the actual distance covered is 39 m. From that point, a shaft 15 m. deep is cut vertically to the level to which a channel from the spring runs.

There is every reason to suppose that this is the method by which the Jebusites had access to the spring in time of war, and that it was the means whereby the capture of the town by David was achieved. The position of the head of the shaft would be inside the town, while the spring would be outside the walls. On this evidence, the position of the east wall of the town could not be that on the crest of the ridge uncovered by a succession of excavations from Warren in 1867 to Macalister in 1923–6, for the head of the tunnel comes to the surface 27 m. outside this wall. In particular, Macalister's ascription of an imposing tower here (pl. 10) to David and Solomon and his interpretation that it was built as a strengthening of the Jebusite wall, to which he ascribed the rougher masonry to the north,[4] could not be correct.

The earliest wall was in fact found at a point 48 m. further

[4] *Macalister*, p. 49 ff., especially p. 57 and fig. facing p. 49.

*Pl. 11. The Jebusite and Davidic wall of Jerusalem from the north.*

east and 27·25 m. lower down. It was revealed at the extreme lower end of the trench cut down the slope by the 1961–7 expedition. The dating evidence was clear. It was originally built c. 1800 B.C. It was still in use in the 8th century B.C., and must therefore have been the wall of the Jebusite town that was captured by David and that was thereafter repaired by him as the wall of his own city.

It was with this wall as a starting point that the plan of Davidic Jerusalem has been worked out. The section of wall first uncovered consisted of a salient projecting forward for a distance of 5 m. from what appeared to be the main line of the wall (pl. 11), though to the north this disappeared very soon beneath a later wall. Such a salient could be part of a wall built in a series of offsets and insets, a form of defensive wall known in the history of Palestinian towns, though the best dated examples are later. Alternatively, it could be the angle of a tower, and it is an attractive theory that this was a gate-tower. The access to the spring Gihon by tunnel and shaft has been described. But this would have been the access in times of danger, and it is inconceivable that there was not a simpler approach at other times. The line is likely to have been very close to that of the present path down to the spring from the summit (pl. 12). Logic therefore demands that there must have been a water-gate, which may have been the main east gate of the town, at approximately this point. Clearance southwards from the portion of the wall exposed in the original trench was therefore undertaken. A total length of 13 m. of the wall was exposed, without any evidence of a gate being found. It was not possible to go any further without cutting the pathway, which would have caused too much inconvenience to the inhabitants to be contemplated. It remains, however, probable that a gate existed closely adjacent to the excavated area.

To the north of the section of the original wall first exposed, the wall disappeared almost immediately beneath the later wall, to be described below (p. 135). Evidence for its further course was derived from three further excavation areas. Site

*Pl. 12. The east slope of the eastern ridge, showing the path which may be near the line of the original approach to the spring.*

H was one of the few sites available on the summit of the ridge which was suitable for excavation. To its south, the whole area had been stripped by earlier excavators, using methods which could not produce scientific evidence. To the north, the area was cut up by houses and narrow strips of garden, which created enormous difficulties for the excavator. Site H itself provided many difficulties. Its area was limited, and down it ran a path to the house at the east end which had to be left open, and also a vital waterpipe. Sufficient area was, however, available for excavation to show that the earliest occupation in the northern part of the site was about the 10th century B.C. This evidence was complemented by that from Site P, a restricted area just to the south. There the picture was quite different. Only the lowest levels were undisturbed, and they clearly belonged to the Late Bronze Age, probably c. 13th century B.C. Between these two areas, c. 3m. apart, therefore, must have run the boundary between the original town and an extension that could not be earlier than about the time of Solomon. This area was in fact largely occupied by a massive wall of several periods, but it lay in the narrow strip between the previous excavations and the path, so its date could not be adequately established. It is nevertheless likely to be in origin

*Pl. 13. The Jebusite and Davidic wall of Jerusalem from the south.*

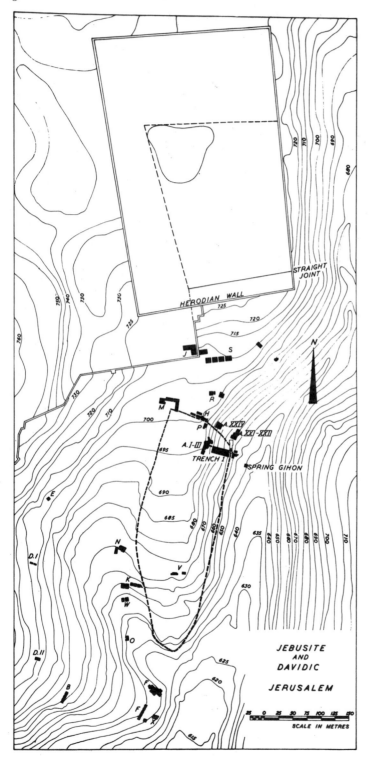

*Fig. 6. Plan of Jebusite and Davidic Jerusalem.*

the north wall of the earliest town. The crest of the hill here is narrow, and it is likely that the wall ran perpendicularly across it to the central valley, for there are no natural features to influence its course.

Square A XXIV was an attempt to pick up the line of the wall running up the hill from the portion exposed towards the base of the line across the summit. This it did not achieve, for the line must have been more oblique than was originally supposed; this was indeed confirmed by further clearance at the foot. A XXIV did however provide very useful confirmatory evidence. The structures found here were completely different from those in the area cleared only some 25 m. to the south, which go back to the Late Bronze Age. The first buildings in A XXIV belong to the 8th–7th centuries B.C., and the original town wall must lie to the south.

The line of the northern and north-eastern part of the walls of the original Jerusalem have therefore been established with reasonable certainty. The continuation to the south of the east wall can only be guessed at, and the plan, fig. 6, suggests that it follows approximately the same contour till it reaches the southern tip of the eastern ridge. A series of soundings, shown on the plan,[5] made it clear that no part of the western side of the western ridge was included in Old Testament Jerusalem. The original wall must therefore have turned back to follow the eastern side of the central valley. No actual portions of the wall have been found, but it is reasonably certain that, in contrast to the east wall, the west wall followed the crest of the summit ridge. The clearest evidence was in Site K. This site lay on a terrace just below the scarp bounding the summit ridge. A little Iron Age pottery was found in clefts in the rock, but there were no structures or occupation of the period, and indeed as clearance was extended westward it was shown that the terrace had been created by massive substructures of the Maccabean period. Site N, 50 m. further north, was further out into the valley, but confirmed that there was no early occupation on the western slopes of the ridge. In Site M, at the north-west corner, the part of the clearance that might have been expected to pick up the line of the wall showed that all deposits here had been removed by later quarrying. The line shown on the plan for the western wall is based on negative evidence only, but there is a high degree of probability that it is correct.

The Jerusalem captured by David is revealed, with all the reservations demanded by the limitations of the evidence, as an elongated triangle, with the east and west sides following the shape of the ridge, the northern base of the triangle crossing it transversely on an arbitrary line. The area enclosed is

[5] Fig. 6, sites B, DI, DII, E.

c. 10·87 acres. This area consisted of two very different parts, a narrow summit plateau, at its widest not much more than 100 m. across, and on the east a slope running steeply down to the central valley. This lopsided development was undoubtedly dictated by the need to control access to the spring. The wall is in fact sited with some skill. In time of war, the inhabitants could obtain their water under cover by means of the tunnel and shaft described above (p. 25 f.). But however carefully the external entrance to the spring was disguised, they could not expect that spies or traitors would not disclose its position to an enemy. The town wall had therefore to be close enough to the spring for the defenders to inhibit or discourage interference with it by attackers. On the other hand, it could not be so low on the slope, and certainly not low enough to enclose the spring, as to bring it under fire from enemies stationed on the eastern side of the Kedron valley. The photograph, pl. 14, shows how near the eastern slope is. Little is known about the range of projectiles available to attackers in the Late Bronze Age and the time of David, consisting presumably of sling-stones and arrows. One probably, in fact, has to argue this from the position of the east wall of the original Jerusalem. Horizontally, this is at a distance of 95 m. from an equivalent point on the east side of the valley. This was pre-

*Pl. 14. The position of the eastern wall, near the foot of the excavated area, in relation to the opposite slope.*

sumably considered to be out of range for the contemporary armament of attackers.

The necessity of bringing the eastern wall far down the slope was recognized by the Middle Bronze Age inhabitants, c. 1800 B.C. The area of this slope enclosed was one difficult to adapt to urban development. The present slope is at an angle of 45°, and that of the underlying bedrock at an angle of 25°. The earliest structures, surviving only fragmentarily, that are contemporary with the original wall, follow this slope. As is to be expected, they are unimpressive, consisting of small and irregular buildings. A break-through in the treatment of this unencouraging area comes in the Late Bronze Age, perhaps c. 13th century B.C. Though the exact date is uncertain owing to the paucity of the evidence, it is certain that the general period is that of the Israelite infiltration into Palestine, in which the strength of the Jebusites in Jerusalem was such that they could repel the invading bands. The archaeological evidence of major town-planning developments accords with the Biblical evidence that Jerusalem was too powerful and virile to succumb in the initial infiltration stage.

The town-planning operations of the Late Bronze Age have been revealed in a limited area, but it is not unreasonable to suppose that they covered the whole area of the eastern slope that was enclosed within the walls. In the area excavated they are most impressive. A system of terraces was built up, with retaining walls parallel to the slope, against which were piled great masses of stones, divided into compartments by thin stabilising walls (pl. 15). The extant height of this fill is 6 m., but there is evidence to suggest that it was originally higher. The full picture of this development is obscured by subsequent erosions and collapses, but it can be envisaged as transforming the steep slope with straggling and irregular buildings into a series of terraces with buildings on a much more substantial scale in the level areas so provided.

One can therefore envisage the town captured by David as a promontary projecting south from the main summit ridge, defended by steep valleys to the east and west, with a north wall crossing the ridge at a point just far enough north to secure access to the vital spring in the eastern valley. This area of c. 10·87 acres was composed of two parts, the narrow summit of the ridge, and the eastern slopes, converted into a usable area by the terracing operations just described. David's preoccupations, having captured the city, are described in I Chronicles 11. 8 and II Samuel 5. 9. His attention to the town walls is nowhere specified; it was perhaps taken for granted. What is specified is his attention to *Millo*. The

*Pl. 15. The stone filling supporting terraces on the steep eastern slope.*

identification of *Millo* has for long been a subject of argument. The meaning of the word is *filling,* but the translators from the Hebrew were so uncertain as to its implication that they transcribed the word as it stood. The present archaeological evidence suggests very strongly that *Millo* was the terrace structure, in the most exact sense a filling, which was the basis of not far from half of the whole town of Jerusalem. The collapse of these terraces, which as will be seen as final at the time of the Babylonian destruction, would deprive the city of a large part of its effective area. The whole structure was certainly vulnerable. Any collapse in the retaining walls, as a result of natural causes such as earthquake or torrential rains, or of destruction by enemies, would let the houses behind them collapse into the valley. The archaeological evidence provides clear examples of such collapses. From the literary evidence, David, Solomon and Hezekiah repaired *Millo* (I Chronicles 11. 8, II Samuel 5. 9, I Kings 9. 24, 11. 27, II Chronicles 32. 5). Such a preoccupation with *Millo* fits well with the archaeological and structural evidence that the terrace structure is to be interpreted as *Millo* and as a constant care of the rulers of Jerusalem.

The literary evidence suggests that David repaired the city that he captured. There is no evidence that he developed it or expanded it. With this the archaeological evidence agrees. Politically, this is entirely reasonable. He was far too deeply involved in conquests, stretching from Damascus in the north to the Gulf of 'Aqaba in the south, to engage in major architectural schemes in his capital. A rationalisation of this for the historian is perhaps to be found in the prohibition by Yahweh that he should build the Temple to house the Ark because he was a man of war and had shed blood.[6] The creation of Jerusalem as a city of splendour, a truly Royal City, belongs to the time of Solomon.

[6] I Chronicles 22. 8, 28. 3.

# 5 &#x2741; SOLOMON'S JERUSALEM

Solomon succeeded his father c. 960 B.C.[1] He succeeded to a kingdom with far-flung rule, and with riches derived from trade to the east and west. This basis of power and riches sharply separates Solomon from the simple tribal background from which David had emerged. For a very short time, the kingdom created by David was a world power, in the context of western Asia at that time. Riches were available, and Solomon used them, and his power over the population, for his capital and for the other Royal Cities. The text of I Kings 9. 15 provides in fact evidence for the conception of the approach to Old Testament history that is suggested by the title of this book. 'And this is the reason of the levy which King Solomon raised; for to build the house of the Lord, and his own house, and Millo, and the wall of Jerusalem, and Hazor, and Megiddo, and Gezer.' The needs of Jerusalem, his capital, came first, but linked with Jerusalem are three other cities which were of especial importance to the king, and these can therefore be called Royal Cities. Such a conception shows how far Israel had advanced towards a secular and a non-tribal monarchy in the forty years since David had united the tribes into a single kingdom.

The needs of Jerusalem were first stated, and no doubt took precedence. The need to repair the defences was obviously important, and if the interpretation of *Millo* is as proposed above, it was equally important. The house of the Lord and the king's house are new. David had not provided in Jerusalem a centre for the cult of Yahweh and for the Ark of the Covenant which was the symbol of Yahweh's resting place. The tribes were perhaps not ready to accept the idea that the central cult symbol that had travelled with them in

[1] There is no close evidence for the dates of David and Solomon.

36

*Pl. 16. The south-east corner of Herod's Temple platform.*

their nomadic days should have a fixed location in a capital that was the king's own property. A rationalisation of the chronicler of this hostility is perhaps to be found in the statement[2] that because David was a man of blood, he was not permitted to build the house of the Lord, and he bequeathed this task to his son, having made preparations for the assembling of the materials.[3] A more prosaic interpretation would be that he had not had time to undertake the task.

The site of the Temple was the threshing floor of Araunah the Jebusite, which was the traditional site at which the plague threatening Jerusalem from the north, and which to the south had extended to Beersheba, was halted by Yahweh's command to the angel of the Lord.[4] In response to the miraculous arrest of the pestilence on the outskirts of Jerusalem, David bought the threshing floor of this Jebusite still dwelling in the vicinity of Jerusalem[5] and erected thereon an altar. This was the site selected by Solomon for the Temple.[6] It is natural for a threshing floor to be outside a town or village. An open space is required, and one to which the wind required for the winnowing has free access. Moreover, the dust from the chaff blown away in the winnowing would be intolerable in a built-up area. It is therefore reasonable to accept the fact that the threshing floor of Araunah the Jebusite was outside the walls of David's city.

Secondly, the site of the Jebusite-Davidic city has been established on the archaeological grounds described in the preceding chapter. The northern boundary of this city is separated by a distance of some 200 m. from the southern wall of the present platform of the Moslem sanctuary of the Haram esh-Sharif. This platform in its present state is quite undoubtedly the work of Herod the Great, in his magnificent rebuilding of the Temple in the last third of the 1st century B.C., for Herod's masonry survives today (pl. 16) to a height

[2] I Chronicles 22. 8–10; I Chronicles 28. 2–3.
[3] I Chronicles 22. 2–6.
[4] II Samuel 24. 16.
[5] II Samuel 24. 24; I Chronicles 21. 25.
[6] II Chronicles 3. 1.

*Pl. 17. South-east corner of Herod's Temple platform, with straight joint between Herodian and earlier masonry.*

*Pl. 18. Detail of straight joint between Herodian and earlier masonry.*

of 128 ft. above its foundations, a height which is approximately that of the present interior surface of the Haram. Between Herod's Temple and that of Solomon, there are no chronological gaps that could allow of any doubt arising as to the site of the Temple. The United Monarchy of David and Solomon was succeeded in the division between north and south by the kingdom of Judah without any serious gap. The kingdom of Judah finally fell to Babylon in 587 B.C. The leaders and rich men were carried away into captivity, but the 'poorest sort of the people of the land' were left behind.[7] There was no absolute depopulation. That the poor remnant did its best to maintain the services in the Temple is shown by the fact that the exiles in Babylon endeavoured to send them offerings to assist them in this duty. The Temple may have been ruinous, but it had not disappeared. When the first exiles were allowed to return by Cyrus, after the Persians had conquered Babylon c. 530 B.C., their first care was to rebuild the Temple. Between this Temple and that built by Herod the Great there was no break. It can therefore be said with confidence that the certain site of the Temple of Herod gives an assured indication of the site of Solomon's Temple. The great courtyard of Herod's Temple, on a platform above the enclosing valleys, was larger than that of its predecessor, for this is the clear statement of Josephus.[8] This platform no doubt envelops its predecessor, and there are therefore uncertainties as to the latter's exact lines, but these uncertainties are minor.

The final season of the 1961–7 excavations, aided by a clearance carried out by the Jordanian Department of Antiquities in 1966, did however furnish suggestive evidence for the interpreting of these uncertainties. The clearance carried out by the Department of Antiquities removed a considerable depth of relatively modern deposit against the eastern face of the south-east corner of the Herodian Temple platform. This revealed that at a distance of 32·72 m. from the south-east corner there was a straight joint in the lower part of the wall (pls. 17 and 18). To the south was the well-known Herodian-type masonry. To the north was drafted masonry of a quite different type and with much heavier bosses; a detailed analysis suggests that there were up to three periods in this masonry. The evidence is inescapable that Herod added this additional 32 m. at the south end of the Temple platform. The masonry visible belongs only to a relatively high part of the great wall supporting the platform, for we know on the evidence of Warren's soundings[9] that bedrock is some 70 ft. lower; Warren, incidentally, recorded this straight joint,[10] but his observation has been ignored by subsequent com-

[7] II Kings 24. 14.
[8] *Wars* I. xxi. 1 ; *Antiquities* XV.xi.1.
[9] Warren. Atlas, pl. XIX.
[10] *Ibid.*

*Pl. 19. Herodian masonry at the Wailing Wall at the west side of the Temple platform.*

mentators. M. Maurice Dunand, well versed in the masonry of Phoenicia, expressed an opinion on visiting the site that the visible masonry north of the straight joint is Persian. This he very convincingly demonstrated to me in a visit to the great Temple of Eshmoun, near Sidon,[11] dated to the late 6th–early 5th century B.C., and to the rather later structures of the Persian period at Byblos.[12] It is thus very tempting to ascribe it to the work of Zerubbabel, who, when the first exiles returned to Jerusalem under the Persian aegis, restored the Temple, completing the restoration c. 515 B.C.[13] One thing can be taken as absolutely certain. Zerubbabel with his meagre resources would not have increased the size of the Temple platform. He could have reduced it, but probably much the easiest thing for him to do would be to rebuild the Solomonic retaining walls. It seems a reasonable assumption, therefore, that this straight joint represents the south-east corner of the Solomonic Temple platform; an ardous, and for the greater part of the depth unrewarding, excavation might reveal at the base Solomonic masonry.

This straight joint has no reflection on the west side of the present platform. There, the Herodian masonry continues for

[11] *Bulletin du Musée de Beyrouth, XVIII, XIX.*
[12] *Ibid.,* XIX.
[13] Ezra 6. 15.

*Pl. 20. The salient in the wall of the Old City, to the south of the Temple platform.*

a distance of at least 185 m. from the south-west corner, where it is revealed in the Wailing Wall area (pl. 19). The implication could be either that the western side of the original platform had been destroyed below the level of the platform walls at present visible, or that the original west wall lay to the east of (inside) the Herodian line.

The archaeological evidence supports the second hypothesis. As seen in pl. 20, the present wall of the Old City breaks off from the Haram (Temple) platform, to form a salient projecting south for a distance of 77 m. The original masonry of the south-east angle of this salient is on a colossal scale, but is not Herodian; it almost certainly belongs to the period of the Roman city of Aelia Capitolina.[14] The origin of the salient is, however, earlier. East of its line, quarrying, which is to be ascribed to the time of Herod the Great's enormous building operations in the last third of the 1st century B.C., respected its line. The most probable interpretation is that this was the line of the city wall from Solomonic down to Maccabean times,[15] and that the line of this wall ran to the south-west corner of the

[14] *P.E.Q.* 1967, p. 70; *P.E.Q.* 1968, pp. 98–102.
[15] *P.E.Q.* 1968, p. 102.

Solomonic Temple platform. If this suggestion is considered on the basis of the physical configuration of the site, it is very convincing. Warren's section (fig. 7) shows Herod's platform spanning the eastern ridge, crossing the central valley, with the west wall based on the opposite slope. A limit for Solomon's platform on the line suggested would neatly crown this eastern ridge. This seems a very reasonable position. An elevation which is hypothetical not only because the limits of the Solomonic platform are deduced rather than observed, but because the contours of the rock can only be estimated, is shown on fig. 8.

*Fig. 7. Elevation of the south wall of the Haram, after Warren, Jerusalem 1867–70, pl. X, A–B.*

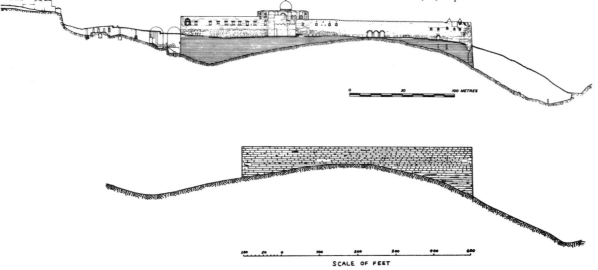

*Fig. 8. Conjectural elevation of the south wall of the platform of Solomon's Temple.*

   It therefore fits all the present evidence, literary and archaeological, that probably Solomon built his Temple with a distance of at least 232 m. between the southern limits of its platform and the northern wall of the city to which he succeeded. With the Temple was associated his Palace.[16] The contours of the spur demanded the the Palace was based on an artificial platform like the Temple, though it could have been at a lower level. One possibility is that it was contained within the area of the present Haram. Another is that much of the area between the Temple and the original north wall, which, as described below, was probably enclosed by an extension of the city walls, was occupied by his palace and ancillary official buildings and that the whole formed a royal quarter, which would be ancestral to that of Samaria, described in Chapter 7. Herodian and Roman quarrying has removed all evidence in the area excavated and very probably in the entire area.

[16] I Kings 6–7.

*Pl. 21. Foundations of a casemate wall at Jerusalem, Site H, possibly belonging to Solomon's extension between the Davidic city and the Temple.*

It would in fact be very likely that when Solomon built his Temple and Palace he joined them to the original city, and enclosed the intervening area within an extension of the city walls. When the first facts began to emerge in the 1961–7 excavations, it was taken as probable that Solomon's extension was from the north-east corner of the original city, low on the eastern slope.[17] This assumption was proved wrong by the completion in 1966 of the excavation of Square A XXIV.[18] This area was shown to have been outside the city until at least the 8th century B.C. Solomon's wall is probably to be recognised in a very fragmentarily preserved casemate wall (pl. 21) running north along the eastern scarp on Site H, of which the significance was not clear when it was first discovered.[19] The plan of Solomon's Jerusalem is given in fig 9, with the reservation that the exact limits of the platform on which stood the Temple and possibly the Palace are unknown. The plan shows it on the lines just suggested.

[17] *P.E.Q.* 1966, pp. 78–80.
[18] *P.E.Q.* 1967, p. 68.
[19] *P.E.Q.* 1963, pp. 17–18.

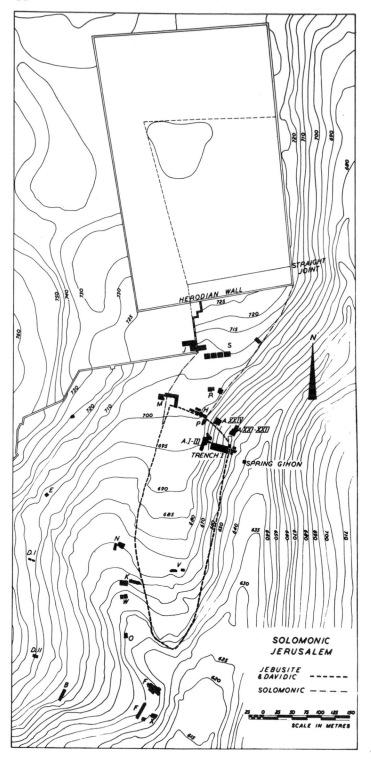

*Fig. 9. Conjectural plan of Solomonic Jerusalem.*

*Pl. 22. Roman quarrying at the south end of the site of the original city.*

The area enclosed therefore consisted of the eastern slopes of the ridge as far north only as was required to control access to the spring, on which the houses were built on the terraces constructed by the Jebusites. Solomon's repair of *Millo* is recorded in 1 Kings 9. 15. The main part of the town lay on the relatively level surface of the ridge. The houses built on the terraces could be expected to have been frequently destroyed because of the artificial and unstable nature of their foundations. The repeated Biblical reports of the rebuildings of *Millo* and the archaeological evidence give full confirmation of this. Nothing of Solomon's city survives here. The houses on the summit, however, could have been founded on solid rock, or at least on consolidated fill above the rock. Here it could have been hoped that at least portions of his buildings would have survived, even if mutilated in subsequent periods. This hope was not fulfilled. It turned out that virtually the whole of the summit of the ridge served as a vast quarry in the Roman period. Old Testament Jerusalem was destroyed by the Romans under Titus in A.D. 70. It lay in ruins until in A.D. 135, after the Second Revolt of the Jews, Hadrian built Aelia Capitolina to obliterate Jewish Jerusalem. Excavations towards the southern end of the eastern ridge showed that occupation came to an end in the last part of the 1st century A.D.,[20] save for some revival in the Byzantine period. Excavation also showed that in this area there were devastating quarrying operations. This is best illustrated in the area cleared by Weill in 1913–14.[21] The whole area cleared consisted of quarries, in part cutting deeply into the rock, in part only partially removing baths, cisterns and cellars of the buildings down to the 1st century A.D. (pl. 22). An excavation in an adjoining area in 1965 showed that at least the first stages of this quarrying

[20] *P.E.Q.* 1963, p. 19.
[21] Weill, *La Cité de David.*

belong to the 2nd century A.D. From this point northward in virtually every area excavated, the rock proved to have been quarried away at some time prior to the Byzantine period. The limit of the quarryings was found to be the salient of the city wall that runs south from the Haram. This can be taken as the limit of Hadrian's Aelia Capitolina. South of this point, the very rock on which original Jerusalem and that of the time of Solomon stood has been carved away to provide building stone for the Roman city.

The three parts of Solomon's Jerusalem have thus suffered different fates. That on the eastern slope has collapsed and disappeared, that of the urban area on the summit has been quarried away, that of the Temple and Palace has been engulfed beneath Herod's greater structure. The result is the same. Not a trace has survived of Solomon's Jerusalem, except for a few indications of the lines of its walls. We are therefore reduced to the literary record for any evidence of the appearance of the first Royal City of the Old Testament.

The description of Solomon's Temple and Palace is given in great detail in I Kings 6–7. As one reads the descriptions, one's impression is that of exotic magnificence, the full significance of which in the culture of Israel can only be appreciated if one remembers how simple were the origins of Solomon's father David. Israel had moved into the class of a world power (in the limited connotation of the period) and there is a certain aspect of the *nouveau riche* about the matter. The plan of the Temple was relatively simple, a porch, a basilical main chamber with a central hall flanked by multi-storeyed side rooms, and at the end the Holy of Holies in which the Ark was housed, never to be seen by profane eyes. It is the ancillaries that are exotic, and even further removed from the conception of the Ark in a tent than is this great permanent structure which was to be the home of this symbol of Yahweh.

The bones of the structures of the Temple were of stones, each so perfectly quarry-dressed that no further dressing on the site was required.[22] But none of this fine mason's work was visible in the interior. The inner face of the walls was covered with cedar carved with birds and flowers, and the interior was floored with cedar.[23] Over the cedarwood of the walls was a veneer of gold,[24] and there was a screen of hanging chains of gold between the Holy of Holies and the main hall.[25] The appearance of the sanctuary is therefore that of an overwhelming ostentation of gold. The character is given by the decorations. The great dim mystery of the Holy of Holies was dominated at its rear wall by two mighty cherubim, half human, half angelic creatures 5 m. in height and with a wing span of 5 m., whose wings met in the centre to offer protection.

[22] I Kings 6. 7.
[23] I Kings 6. 16.
[24] I Kings 6. 20–21.
[25] I Kings 6. 21.

to the Ark.[26] The cherubim were carved in olive-wood and overlaid with gold. The walls of the main hall and the doors were also carved with cherubim and with palm trees and flowers.

The altar of the Temple was overlaid with gold, and on it stood ten candlesticks of pure gold, as were the various accessories, bowls, snuffers, basins, spoons and censers.[27] On the east side of the Temple were five tables covered with gold.[28]

Outside the Temple were fitments and cult accessories of 'bright brass', presumably bronze, cast in the Jordan valley. There was a bronze-plated altar, with a 'molten sea' 5 m. across, supported on twelve oxen and carved with lilies, in which the priests could wash themselves after making sacrifices, and for washing the offerings were ten bronze basins on wheeled carriages 2 m. across, carved with lions, oxen and cherubim.[29] Most spectacular of all were two pillars of bronze, according to I Kings 7. 15–16, $11\frac{1}{2}$ m. high, including the capitals; according to II Chronicles 3. 15, 20 m. high. The cast bronze capitals were ornamented with basket work and wreathed with chains from which hung bronze pomegranates. The top of the capitals were lily-shaped. The purpose of the pillars, called Jachin and Boaz, is obscure, for they were not apparently structural. They must have had a cult significance, perhaps allied to that of the standing stones of the Canaanite religion.

One can in general visualise the Temple from the description. It must, like its Herodian successor, have stood on a platform supported by high retaining walls rising from the slopes of the valleys to east and west, for only thus could the narrow surface of the ridge have been extended to provide the necessary space. On this stood the Temple building, with a total length of 76 m. and a height of 15 m. The external appearance and the architectural details are described in much less detail than the interior and the fitments. It is possible to suggest a number of alternative reconstructions, and for none of them is there conclusive evidence. This does not really matter very much, for the vivid description of the interior can be interpreted in the light of the cultural setting of Solomon's Jerusalem.

The key to this exotic building amongst a people not many generations removed from the austerities and simplicities of nomadic life is that Solomon sent to Hiram King of Tyre not only for cedar and fir-wood from the forest of Lebanon but for the craftsmen to work the wood and masons to dress the stone. The head masons or craftsmen no doubt included the architect, just as they did in medieval England, though one can only guess at the specifications and details laid down by

[26] I Kings 6. 23–28.
[27] I Kings 7. 48–51.
[28] II Chronicles 4. 8.
[29] I Kings 7. 23–39.

*Pl. 23. Ivory carving from Nimrud, illustrating the probable style of the decoration of Solomon's Temple.*

*Pl. 24. Ivory carving from Nimrud.*

*Pl. 25. Bronze stand for laver from Cyprus.*

Solomon in commissioning the work. Solomon was thus importing into his capital the culture of Phoenicia, a country far richer than Palestine, and in direct contact with the full civilisation of the eastern Mediterranean and western Asia. One can therefore justly interpret the Biblical descriptions of the structure, the ornaments and the fittings in the light of archaeological evidence of the culture of this area. The evidence for the mason's work will be discussed in connection with the later Royal City of Samaria, where it has been shown that Phoenician craftsmen were also employed. Samaria also provides a valuable link for the style of art in the decoration, which is part of a widespread Syro-Phoenician complex. All that has survived at Samaria is on a small scale, the decoration in ivory of panels or of furniture. But the description of the ornamentation of the wall of the Temple immediately invites comparison with the similar small-scale ivories found in the palace of Assur-Nasir-pal at Nimrud. This palace was completed in 879 B.C., but the ivories as a collection probably date to the time of Sargon II and were deposited c. 715 B.C., many of them loot from the western provinces (pl. 23). Magnified many times these can convey an impression of the cherubim, the plants and the animals that ornamented the Holy of Holies and the main hall of the Temple. No close parallels can be suggested for the pillars Jachin and Boaz, though their decoration is in the same artistic style, but parallels for the basins on wheels can be produced from Megiddo and Cyprus, and reconstructions of the great 'molten sea' supported by twelve oxen can be suggested in terms of contemporary art.

Only two positive architectural elements can be added to this picture as a result of the excavations. A proto-Ionic pilaster capital was found fallen from the summit scarp adjacent to the original north wall of the city. Such capitals occur in association with buildings of the early monarchy. Secondly, in excavations along the line of the wall which it was expected would join the Temple to the original north wall was found a wall of 8th-century B.C. date in which were re-used stones of Phoenician type, which may have been derived from Solomon's wall (pl. 27). Both these points will be discussed in conjunction with the Samaria evidence of Phoenician building.

All this was designed as the trappings of the home of the Ark that had hitherto been housed in a simple tabernacle or tent. This was the great revolution of Solomon's Jerusalem. To the ordinary Bronze Age–Iron Age town of Jerusalem, captured and preserved unaltered by David, and to an Israelite culture in comparison with which Jebusite Jerusalem was civilised, Solomon added this fixed temple for Yahweh, with all the trappings of the much more civilised culture of Phoenicia, heathen though it must have seemed to the adherents of the austere Yahweh cult.

The original town of Jerusalem was thus in the time of

*Pl. 26. Bronze stand for laver from Megiddo.*

*Pl. 27. Wall at Jerusalem, Site S II, containing re-used stones probably of Solomonic date.*

Solomon dominated by the site of the Temple, higher up the ridge, and made more dominating by the structure of the artificial platform required to provide the space for the building itself and the associated courts. The ordinary Semitic High Place was outside the towns, and temples within a town may be an alien conception. It is suggested above (p. 43) that when the Temple was built, the area between it and the original north wall was enclosed. The archaeological evidence, as so far evaluated, is not sufficiently precise to prove this point, but it makes it probable, and the plan (fig. 9) is drawn on these lines. It is at least certain that by the 8th century B.C. the town and Temple were so linked. But it could be possible that originally the Temple was a separate, acropolis-like enclosure.

In the Biblical account, the building of Solomon's Palace is linked with that of the Temple. Its cost was defrayed from the same levy[30] and the account of its building, in I Kings 7. 1–12, comes in the middle of the description of the Temple. It may be inferred that the construction of the Temple and Palace was consecutive rather than simultaneous, since in I Kings 6. 48–7. 1, it is said that Solomon was occupied in building the Temple for seven years and the Palace for thirteen years, while in I Kings 9. 10 the total period of building 'the two houses, the house of the Lord, and the King's house' is given as twenty years. The Palace was certainly elaborately built of expensive materials, as was the Temple, though the emphasis is more on elaborate masonry rather than on gold plating. The description of the Palace is not given in much detail. The first element mentioned[31] is the 'house of the forest of Lebanon'; there is no indication of how it was connected with the rest of the Palace, and it could even, from the phrasing, have been a detached building. It was a great hypostyle hall 50 m. long by 25 m. wide·and 15 m. high. The roof of cedarwood was supported by forty-five pillars of cedarwood;[32] from this no doubt came the name 'house of the forest of Lebanon'. Along the sides were three tiers of windows. The description of the main part of the Palace begins[33] with a porch of pillars, 25 m. long by 15 m. wide. Next in the description comes the 'porch for the throne where he might judge, even the porch of judgement'.[34] Next comes the 'house where he dwelt',[35] but all that is said of it was that it had a court. It might be inferred that the public rooms of the Palace were well known, but that the writer and those from whom he drew his information were not familiar with the king's private quarters. For an interpretation of what the Palace was like, it is permissible to draw on evidence of comparable palaces of the 10th–9th centuries on Phoenicia-Syria, from which area so much of Solomon's architectural inspiration was derived.[36]

[30] I Kings 9. 15.
[31] I Kings 7. 2–5.
[32] In I Kings 7. 2 said to be in four rows, whereas in 7. 3, three rows are implied.
[33] I Kings 7. 6.
[34] I Kings 7. 7.
[35] I Kings 7. 8.
[36] This interpretation is well discussed in *I.E.J.* 16. by Ussishkin. I am indebted for a number of suggestions to this article.

From the Biblical description, it can be inferred that the public approached Solomon's audience chamber, in which was situated his throne, through a 'porch of pillars', presumably a portico with an entrance supported on pillars. This would accord well with the *bit-ḥilani* type of plan, of which palaces at Sencherli give examples.[37] The *bit-ḥilani* type of plan is characterised by entrances on the long side of rooms; an interpretation on such lines would suggest that a wide portico, with an entrance supported on pillars, approached the long side of Solomon's audience chamber, at one end of which was his throne. From the audience chamber, Solomon would retire to the courtyard whence opened his private apartments; for them we can produce no planning evidence. It is suggested below[38] that Building 1723 at Megiddo, one of Solomon's constructions, shows on a smaller scale a similar sort of layout.

As has already been quoted, beyond the entrance porch lay the porch for the throne. The Syrian examples provide evidence for an emplacement for the throne, or of a brazier in front of the probable position. Solomon's throne was of great magnificence.[39] It was said to be of ivory. This may be doubted. Ivory on a scale to form the structural elements of a throne is very improbable. Much more likely is that the structural elements were veneered in ivory.[40] But even such a refined material as ivory was overlaid with pure gold. The throne was raised on six steps and there was a footstool of gold. Flanking the arms of the throne were two lions, and there were said to be twelve lions on each side of the throne standing on the six steps. Twenty-four lions in the round would have indeed been impressive. A more probable interpretation is that on the flanking walls above the steps there was a façade of lions forming a veneer on the walls behind the throne. All the existing evidence for such decoration suggests that this was the method.[41]

Though the description of the building of the Palace is so closely linked with that of the Temple, it is nowhere actually said that it was part of the same complex, though this is usually assumed. Two lines of reasoning may support this assumption. Solomon built a separate palace for Pharaoh's daughter, obviously his principal wife.[42] She, as a follower of a foreign religion, had to have a home which had apparently to be neither in the Davidic city nor associated with the Temple. 'My wife shall not dwell in the house of David King of Israel, because the places are holy, whereunto the Ark of the Lord hath come.' This suggests that his own Palace was too closely associated with the Temple for it to be acceptable that a foreign princess should live there. Secondly, to have built

[37] *Sendschirli IV,* pl. L.
[38] On the lines proposed in *I.E.J.* 16 by Ussishkin.
[39] II Chronicles 9. 17–19.
[40] See below, p. 89.
[41] See especially *Nimrud.*
[42] I Kings 7.8.

his Palace within the original city would have taken up a very great deal of the exiguous space there. The idea of a town dominated by a great royal quarter belongs to the next century, and is discussed below (p. 74 ff). Solomon's Palace is much more likely to have been outside the original city. To this extent it would have been linked with the Temple, though there is no evidence to show whether it was on the same platform or a subsidiary one to the south.

As has already been stressed, the archaeological evidence for Solomon's Jerusalem is regrettably slight. Archaeological evidence for the culture of Phoenicia and the neighbouring countries does, however, provide a visual interpretation for the literary evidence of Solomon's buildings at Jerusalem. The general picture is clear. A simple town on a site in itself unfavourable to grandiose architecture was captured by David, and there is nothing in the literary or archaeological evidence to suggest that he did more than repair it. To this Solomon added buildings, the Temple, his Palace, and the palace of his principal wife, in a style using all the most exotic elements of the more advanced civilisations of Phoenicia and Syria. From the physical configuration of the site, the Temple dominated Jerusalem, either linked to the original town by a narrow extension along the summit of the ridge, which is the preferred interpretation, or, less probably, as a separate, acropolis-type, enclosure. This was Solomon's Royal City of Jerusalem.

# 6 ✦ SOLOMON'S OTHER ROYAL CITIES

A special status is given to three other towns, Hazor, Megiddo and Gezer, by the fact that they are linked with Jerusalem in the passage from I Kings 9. 15 already quoted (p. 36) as sites where work was to be financed by the same levy. It is reasonable to regard them as cities for which the king had special responsibilities, and thus as Royal Cities. Archaeological discoveries have supported this interpretation.

One fact particularly links Megiddo and Hazor. Both were the sites of ancient cities, but at both there was a destruction, in the 13th–12th centuries B.C., followed by a gap in occupation. Though there may have been some slight preceding occupation, Solomon virtually re-established them as cities. It is especially notable that there is no Biblical record of the capture of Megiddo. It slides unannounced into the sphere of the Israelite kingdom. This very strongly suggests that it was abandoned and in ruins at the time at which David's power was being asserted. Hazor likewise had been destroyed, in the 13th century B.C. on archaeological evidence, and was ruinous at the time of the establishment of David's kingdom. For Gezer, the archaeological evidence is at present incomplete. But even if it had remained a flourishing city until the 10th century B.C., it was a Canaanite city, and it came into Solomon's possession after an Egyptian Pharaoh of the 21st Dynasty had captured it, and gave it to Solomon as a dowry for his daughter when she became Solomon's chief wife.[1]

These three cities, therefore, share the characteristic that they were not the property of either the southern or the northern tribes, just as Jerusalem was excluded from the tribal complex, since it was David's personal conquest from

[1] I Kings 9. 16.

53

0        100        200        300 M.

*Pl. 28. Air view of Hazor.*

the Jebusites. The king could therefore treat them as his own property, and was responsible for their development and defence. Because of their strategic importance, he used the levy for their rebuilding and especially for their defences.

The site which has provided the clearest evidence, and which has helped to interpret the evidence from the others, is Hazor, which was excavated by Professor Yigael Yadin between 1955 and 1959. It is situated in northern Palestine, at the eastern foot of the mountains of Galilee, where they slope down to the Jordan valley, and 25·5 km. north of the Sea of Galilee. The site is an enormous one, covering in all 183 acres. As the air photograph shows (pl. 28), the overall plan is L-shaped. The photograph also shows that in the south-west corner of the L is a comparatively small area covering only c. 26 acres, rising appreciably above the plateau of the rest of the site. This was the original nucleus of the town, the real *tell* built up by human occupation, and dating apparently to the Early Bronze Age in the 3rd millennium B.C., though the lower levels have so far hardly been touched in the excavations. To it was added in the second part of the Middle Bronze Age, probably late 18th century B.C., the great plateau to the north, defended by a massive bank, probably originally crowned by a wall, a type of defence claimed to be characteristic of invading warlike bands known as the Hyksos.[2]

Hazor at this stage of maximum expansion and even earlier was certainly a place of great importance. It is mentioned in Egyptian records in the 19th century B.C.[3] and in the Middle and Late Bronze Ages it is mentioned in letters from the Syrian kingdom of Mari and several times in the records of the New Kingdom of Egypt.[4] In the Amarna letters, dealing with the time when raiders were endangering Egyptian control of Palestine, in which Jerusalem also appears,[5] Hazor was one of the cities accused of allying with the infiltrating Habiru.[6]

The latest Egyptian reference to Hazor dates to the 13th century B.C.[7] At this point we arrive at the stage of the Israelite infiltration into Palestine. Hazor is claimed as one of the cities destroyed by Joshua. Joshua 11 describes the alliance led by Jabin king of Hazor against the Israelites, and its defeat by Joshua by the waters of Merom. The climax is described in Joshua 11. 10–11: 'And Joshua at that time turned back and took Hazor, and smote the king thereof with the sword: for Hazor beforetime was the head of all those kingdoms. And they smote all the souls that were therein with the edge of the sword, utterly destroying them: there was not any left to breathe: and he burnt Hazor with fire.'

Modern scholarship would hesitate to ascribe to Joshua all the conquests attributed to him in the Biblical account. That

[2] *Amorites and Canaanites*, pp. 65–73.
[3] G. Posener, *Princes et Pays d'Asie et Nubie,* p. 73. Bruxelles. 1940.
[4] For references, see *Hazor I*, p. 4.
[5] J. A. Knudtzon, *Die El-Amarna Tafeln*, Leipzig, 1915, Nos. 287, 289, 290.
[6] *Ibid.*, Nos. 148, 227, 228; *Antiquités Orientales du Louvres*, 7094.
[7] J. B. Pritchard, *Ancient Near Eastern Texts,* 2nd edition, 1955, p. 477.

account is a conflation, but weight must be attached to the accounts of individual successes by the infiltrating Israelites. The excavations of Hazor have shown that the town of the Middle and Late Bronze Ages was destroyed in the 13th century B.C. A close assessment of the date must await the full publication of the evidence. But it is clear that there was a disastrous destruction within that century, and the Biblical evidence suggests that the Israelites may have been responsible for it. From the archaeological evidence it is clear that this destruction was followed by abandonment, completely final as regards the great northern plateau area, and for some three centuries for the area of the original settlement, the *tell*.

Hazor, therefore, provided the prerequisite already suggested (p. 36) for a Solomonic Royal City. Abandoned since a destruction during the time of the Israelite infiltration, it was not within any tribal control. The importance of the site no doubt took on new life with David's expansionist policy in the direction of the kingdom of Damascus. The extent of some slight re-occupation of the site during the 11th–10th century B.C. has still to be assessed by further excavation. But it is already quite clear that Hazor became a place of importance again in one single and dramatic operation. Solomon made it one of his Royal Cities, by constructing on the original *tell* a

*Pl. 29. Air view of Solomonic gate at Hazor.*

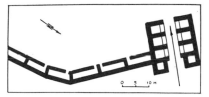

*Fig. 10. Solomonic gate and casemate wall at Hazor.*

royal quarter with defences on a style that other sites show to have been classic.

Solomon's city occupied only a minute proportion of the area of the Bronze Age city. A superficial view would suggest that the original Early Bronze town was oval in shape and included the whole of the bottom bar of the L; this is conjecture only, for the eastern tip of the bar has not been excavated. The contours as seen in pl. 28 suggest that only the western half of this base bar of the L was re-occupied in the Iron Age. The excavation evidence makes it quite clear that there was a marked division between the western half of this re-occupation area and the eastern half. The air photograph (pl. 28) shows an area of excavation in the centre of the higher area. Across this from north to south ran a line of defensive walls, enclosing the area to the west, and cutting it off from the east. Little is so far known about this area to the east, though it is said to have been closely built up.[8] The area to the west contained monumental buildings. The picture is still incomplete, but a great pillared hall, interpreted as a storehouse, existed at later stages just west of the defences running across the mound.

All the evidence available suggests that when Solomon resurrected Hazor as a city, he reserved and defended one section as a separate royal quarter. The defences that cross the Hazor mound from north to south, and turn west to enclose the western part of the *tell*, have been clearly established by the excavations. They consist of casemates, which have an overall width of 5 m., within which were narrow rooms with their longer axis parallel to the walls; that at above ground level they served as rooms is clear from the evidence of doorways at an internal angle of each casemate. This casemated form of wall has in it a magnificent gateway, providing access from the outer areas on the east to the official area to the west. In plan it has a long ancestry in western Asia: One can even interpret it in terms of British archaeology of the Iron Age, an in-turned entrance with guardrooms. But, as will be seen, Solomon's architects interpreted these defensive requirements with a marked individuality and expertise.

The Hazor gate, of which the plan with the adjacent casemates is shown on fig. 10, is well seen on pl. 29. Projecting out from the line of the wall, and presumably from the gate itself, were two towers. These guarded an entrance 4·50 m. wide. This entrance passage was flanked by three guardrooms on each side. The structure was destroyed to the top of its foundations, but presumably the walls seen in the photograph flanking the entrance passage were only sleeper walls, not carried up above ground level.

[8] *Hazor II*, p. 15. Prof. Yadin's more recent results have shown that Solomon's town was confined to the western half of the mound. The following paragraphs must be slightly revised as a result.

The picture presented by Hazor, to the extent that it has so far been revealed by excavation, is clear. The Solomonic city was limited in extent as compared with its Bronze Age predecessors. Half of this area was enclosed by a defensive wall of casemate plan, dividing it from the rest of the reoccupied area, and in this wall was an imposing gateway. It is probable that at this first stage only this area was defended. Within the area thus defended there are indications, still to be confirmed by more complete excavation, that there were buildings of an official character. It seems very likely that one can interpret Solomon's Hazor as a royal quarter. The extent to which there was a subsidiary town to the east has still to be determined.

The Hazor identification of the Solomonic defences and gate drew immediate attention to the so-called Stratum IV gateway at Megiddo on the north side of the mound.[9] The immediate impression of resemblance was indeed so great that, as the first elements of the Hazor gate began to emerge, Professor Yadin gave instructions to excavate the remainder of the area on the assumption that the full plan would correspond with that of the Megiddo gate, and it did.

This gate was correctly assigned by the original excavators[10] to the Solomonic period. But for many years there have been doubts about assigning the whole of Megiddo Stratum IV, with its stables, to the Solomonic period.[11] The stables, as will be seen, belong to a period nearly a century later than that of Solomon. A great step forward in the ascription of the other buildings came when Professor Yadin, determined to deal with the anomalies that the Hazor evidence emphasized, carried out a lightning campaign of only three days in 1960.[12] This firm evidence at Hazor that the Solomonic gateway was associated with the casemate wall made him suspicious that at the same time, with the same defensive criteria and the same military engineers, a gateway at Megiddo identical to that at Hazor should be built in connection with a solid wall constructed with a succession of alternating salients and recesses, an 'offsets and insets' wall, in contrast with the casemate wall at Hazor.

Professor Yadin's investigation was carried out in an area c. 50 m. east of the gateway. He found that the 'offsets and insets' wall was preceded by a casemate wall, not recorded in the earlier excavations. This wall flanked a monumental building, to which Yadin gives the name 'Northern Fort', of which the outer wall formed part of the defences. This monumental building underlay a stable building, 407 of the original Stratum IV plan.[13] The finds in the occupation layer on the floors of the casemates and monumental structure compare closely with those above the Solomonic structures at Hazor.

[9] *M II*, fig. 389.
[10] *M I*, pp. 59–61.
[11] See J. W. Crowfoot, *P.E.Q.* 1940; *SS 3*, pp. 200–4.
[12] *B.A.*, XXIII, p. 62 ff.
[13] *M I*, fig. 49.

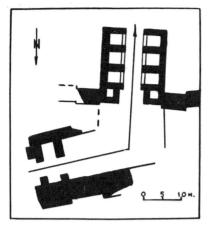

*Fig. 11. Solomonic gate at Megiddo.*

There are gaps in the evidence. The casemate walls have not been traced up to the gateway. The certain contemporaneity of the monumental building with the casemates, which are built against it, has not been proved. The pottery evidence is that of the final occupation, which could bridge successive building periods. But the overall picture is very convincing. Solomon's defences at Megiddo consisted of a most impressive gateway, with which was associated a wall built on the casemate plan, incorporated in which was a monumental structure of official, if not necessarily fortress, type.

The gate[14] is in plan almost identical with that at Hazor, and Yadin's ascription of the two to the same builders cannot be doubted. The two projecting towers of the Hazor gate are represented by solid podia, but these can certainly be interpreted as the base of towers. The sleeper walls crossing the entrances of the guardrooms are not shown, and only kerbs divide the rooms from the entrance passage, but in both, in effect, the guardrooms were open to the passage, and the sleeper walls may well have existed at Megiddo, below the level of the floor. In the Hazor plan, the two towers project beyond the flanking casemate walls. At Megiddo there is so far no evidence, but the other similarities of lay-out are so similar that it is tempting to expect the same planning at Megiddo but by error the line has not been so shown in fig. 14, which is an attempt to indicate what is known of Solomon's Megiddo.

The Megiddo gate adds two important elements to the evidence of the buildings of Solomon's Royal Cities. The first is that the gate through the main wall had outside it an outer gate. The plan[15] shows an oblique approach from the north–east, running up the steep side of the mound that had grown up as a result of the occupation deposits of millennia. Just short of where this oblique approach turned sharply to enter the main gate was an outer gate with an entrance passage approximately the same width as that in the inner gateway, flanked by two pairs of buttresses bounding guardrooms of unequal depth. The interpretation of the outer gateway has not been re-investigated in the light of Professor Yadin's evidence of the character of the defences associated with the original gateway. It is likely that in its final form it belongs to the period of the 'offsets and insets' wall, for the outer supporting wall has this same character. But the plan as drawn suggests two separate elements, and it is plausible that the original outer gate belongs to the casemate defences. A spectacular 'pedestrian staircase' suggested by the excavators as a short-cut to the oblique main approach[16] now appears to belong to a pre-Solomonic phase, and to lead to a water pool.[17]

[14] Shown on *M II,* fig. 389, with the 'offsets and insets' wall and other later structures. Here fig. 11.
[15] *M II,* fig. 389
[16] *M II,* figs. 123, 124.
[17] *I.E.J.* 17, p. 121.

*Pl. 30. Solomonic masonry in gateway at Megiddo.*

*Pl. 31. Solomonic gateway at Megiddo with later blocking.*

*Pl. 32. Solomonic gateway at Megiddo after removal of blocking.*

The second piece of evidence provided by the Megiddo gate concerns the type of masonry. The actual masonry of the defences of Hazor was undistinguished. Almost nothing survived above ground level and the surviving remains were of rough undressed stones. At Megiddo, the foundations are of a different character and some of the superstructure of the gate survives. The Samaria evidence is a guide to the interpretation of the masonry.[18] In the superstructures, the stones are dressed flat with a beautiful finish; in foundations, or in more massive walls, the stones have a flat, well-dressed margin on some sides, but an irregular boss. The gateway provides an excellent illustration of this masonry (pls. 30–32). This is the masonry in use in the Omri-Ahab period at Samaria, when it has been shown[19] that Phoenician masons were employed. As an echo of Solomon's use of Phoenician craftsmen, the evidence from Megiddo is entirely convincing.

The evidence from Professor Yadin's 1960 excavations that the 'offsets and insets' wall had a casemate predecessor, which a strong presumption suggests was associated with the original stage of the Stratum IV gate, has an important bearing on the history of the so-called palace building 1723[20] on the south side of the mound. This was a monumental building, set in a courtyard 59 m. from north to south and 57 m. from east to west. This was attributed by the excavators[21] to the time of David or the early Solomonic period. But it was destroyed by the 'offsets and insets' wall, which the excavators ascribed to Solomon. The destruction by Solomon of an important

[18] See p. 74 ff.
[19] *SS 1*, pp. 5–8.
[20] *M I*, fig. 12.
[21] *M I*, p. 59

building either built by his father or in his own early building operations has for long created a difficulty for those seeking to interpret the excavation results. Professor Yadin's evidence that the 'offsets and insets' wall does not belong to the Solomonic lay-out makes a reasonable interpretation much easier.

It can therefore be accepted that this important building belongs to the Solomonic period; its correspondence with Professor Yadin's 'Northern Fort' may well be the correct interpretation. The building was destroyed to its foundations (pl. 33), with the exception of two or three stones. These stones, however, were sufficient to show, in their size and in their drafting, that the masonry was similar to the Phoenician masonry at Samaria, of the heavier type with bosses and irregular margins. The width of the walls and the depth of the foundations shows the scale of the building and suggests that there were upper storeys.

The walls of this building were destroyed so low that there were no indications of doorways, and indeed even the floors are said to have disappeared. The interpretation of the plan is therefore difficult, and any suggestions can only be hypothetical. The excavators suggested that the wing projecting to the east, 1728 (fig. 12), was a porch, and that the building centred round a tower at M, with the masonry block in the centre forming the core of a staircase. A recent study with a

*Pl. 33. 'Palace' 1723 at Megiddo.*

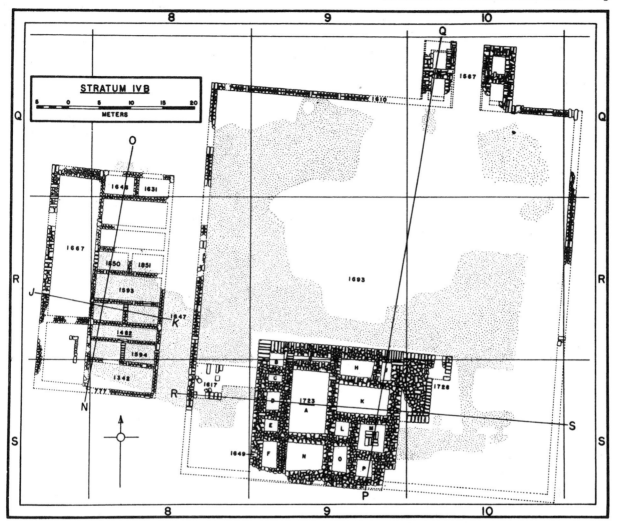

Fig. 12. Plan of Megiddo 'palace' 1723.

divergent interpretation is, however, very plausible.[22] It is based on a study of current palace plans in Syria and in the area of the neo-Hittite Empire, of the *bit-ḥilani* type. The essential element of this was a wide porch approaching the long side of a hall, which was a throne-room or hall or audience.[23] The interpretation suggested in this article is shown on fig. 13; the doorways as shown are admittedly arbitrary. The basic proposal is that room H was a columned portico, for which the Syrian examples provide ample parallels, leading into the long side of the main room K, which would have been where the king or his governor held audiences. This would form the public part of the building. From it a doorway must, on any interpretation, have led into area A, which must, again on any interpretation, have been an open court. Area A is fringed by a number of rooms, mostly

[22] D. Ussishkin, 'King Solomon's Palace and Building 1723 in Megiddo', *I.E.J.* 16

[23] *Op. cit.* for typical plans.

on a small scale, though with massive walls proving that there were upper storeys. These would have formed the residential area. The article suggests that it could even be deduced that there were two separate sets of apartments, at the first floor separately approached, for the king, or governor, and his spouse, for area G is too narrow to have been anything except a staircase, and area M could certainly have been a staircase of newel type, though the article suggests that, since the walls have no extra thickness, it cannot have been a tower, as the excavators had suggested.[24] This interpretation is attractive and plausible, as has already been said. Reference has already been made to an interpretation of the literary evidence for Solomon's Palace at Jerusalem on similar comparative evidence.

Excavation has not revealed the relationship of 'palace' 1723 to the casemate wall. If this is similar to that of Yadin's 'Northern Fort', the casemate wall would have abutted the southern wall of the building, which would, as in Yadin's area, have been approximately on the line of the 'offsets and insets' wall that succeeded it. It is so shown on the tentative plan on fig. 14.

The 'palace' 1723 is shown on fig. 12 as set in a wide court-yard, floored with pounded lime-mortar, though it is noted that this was mostly destroyed, so that stratification, even as inadequately recorded, is not reliable. This courtyard is approached by a gateway in the north-east corner, and it is one of the merits of the interpretation just discussed that this

*Pl. 34. Gateway to courtyard of 'palace' 1723 at Megiddo.*

*Fig. 13. Suggested reconstruction of plan of Megiddo 'palace' 1723.*

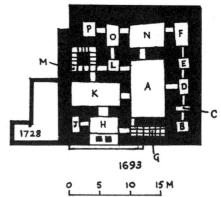

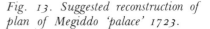

[24] *M I*, p. 23.

*Pl. 35. Piers of ashlar in wall of courtyard of 'palace' 1723.*

*Pl. 36. Piers of ashlar in wall of courtyard.*

would approach more directly to a portico in room H than to the excavator's suggested porch in the projection 1728. The structure of the gateway projects forward from the enclosure walls, with two rooms on either side. As pl. 34 shows, it was constructed of the bossed type of Phoenician masonry; two courses of this survived as seen in the photograph, the lowest course being clearly foundational. The rest of the enclosure wall is in a different type of masonry (pls. 35 and 36). Most of

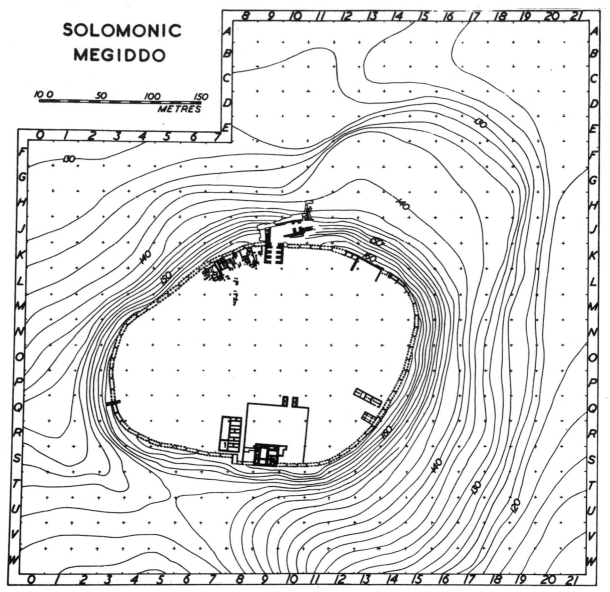

Fig. 14. Tentative reconstruction of the plan of Solomonic Megiddo.

the wall is of very rough rubble, very roughly coursed, but at intervals there are curious 'piers' of ashlar, arranged header-stretcher-header in successive courses. The style of building is also employed in the stables, which, as will be seen, are certainly post-Solomonic, and it has been shown[25] that in them the ashlar blocks are re-used from earlier buildings. It is probable, therefore, that the enclosure wall was rebuilt at a later period, but the gateway and the probability that the 'palace' 1723 would have a spacious setting make it reasonable that there was an original wall on the line of the later one.

[25] Kenyon, *Megiddo, Hazor, Samaria and Chronology*, pp. 149–50.

Adjoining the courtyard to the west, and aligned on it, was a second building, 1482, of considerable size and obviously official character. It was curtailed when the stables were built, so certainly belongs to the Solomonic lay-out. The few fragments of the superstructure that survived were of ashlar blocks, and though these are not illustrated or described in detail it can be taken that the masonry was of the same character as the rest of the structures of the period. The building was presumably administrative. The large enclosure 1667 may have been a hall, or, as the excavators suggest, a porch. The other rooms may have been offices, or may have been living quarters for officials.

The buildings of Solomonic Megiddo so far described have been public. The ascription of the excavators of the whole of Stratum IV, including the great stable compounds, has been proved both on structural evidence and that of stratigraphical evidence of the associated pottery to be post-Solomonic.[26] These buildings over most of the summit of the mound succeed Stratum V, which is divided into two distinct building levels, Vb and Va, both of similar undistinguished small houses. My own view[27] is that the Vb houses belong to the Solomonic period, and that the Va houses were a rebuilding, on unrelated lines, after a destruction by Shishak I c. 930 B.C. Professor Yadin's view is that it is Stratum Va that is to be associated with Solomon.[28] Since his conclusions are more closely related to observations on the site, the tentative plan of Solomonic Megiddo (fig. 14) uses the plan of the Va structures. In giving an impression of the site at the period, the point is not of great significance; a considerable part of the summit of the mound was occupied by small and unimportant buildings; between Vb and Va the actual plan was different, but the character the same.

The conclusion, therefore, is that Solomon imposed on the summit of his Royal City of Megiddo fortifications and a magnificent gateway and a number of buildings of official character. The rest of the summit, however, to the extent for which there was evidence from excavation, was occupied by private buildings. Solomon, therefore, did not establish an *exclusive* royal quarter.

One further aspect of Solomon's activities at Megiddo has still to be mentioned. The Megiddo water system is very famous. Its climax was a great shaft leading down to a tunnel at the south-west corner of the mound. This had been preceded by a sunken gallery leading to the same springs. The excavators ascribed the whole complex to the 12th century B.C., a period when all assessment of the evidence suggests that Megiddo was in a state of decline. Professor Yadin's new

[26] *B.A.* XXIII, 2; *SS 3*, pp. 199–204.
[27] Kenyon, *Megiddo, Hazor, Samaria and Chronology*, p. 151.
[28] *B.A.* XXIII, 2, p. 67.

*Pl. 37. Jamb of gateway at Gezer.*

investigations show that the sunken gallery is likely to belong to the time of Solomon,[29] and therefore that the whole sequence of approaches to the spring belongs to the time of Solomon and to the succeeding kingdom of Israel.

We now come to the last of Solomon's Royal Cities, Gezer. Gezer lies at the western foot of the hill country of Palestine, just before the flattening-out into the coastal plain. This coastal plain for millennia provided the route for contacts between the great empires of Egypt and Mesopotamia. Gezer, with its control over this coastal route, was therefore of permanent importance to Egypt. It is a tribute to Solomon's status (and perhaps also an indication of the low ebb of Egyptian power) that Gezer was given to Solomon as a dowry with Pharaoh's daughter.[30] But from the point of view of Solomon's policy, this was a personal possession, over which none of the tribes of Israel had control. He therefore devoted to it part of the product of his levy.[31]

The excavation of Gezer was one of the earliest large-scale excavations in Palestine, being carried out from 1902 to 1905 and 1907 to 1909. It was excavated with the greatest care by Professor R. A. G. Macalister, and the results were very fully published.[32] But though the first steps in stratigraphical excavation had been taken in England at that time, and though Petrie at T. Hesi had introduced in Palestine a basic conception of excavating a *tell* built up by structures mainly of mudbrick,[33] the evolution of technique was quite inadequate to

[29] *I.E.J.* 16, pp. 279–80; *I.E.J.* 17 pp. 120–1.
[30] I Kings 9. 16.
[31] I Kings 9. 15.
[32] *Gezer I–III.*
[33] Petrie, *Tell el Hesy.*

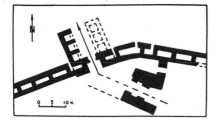

*Fig. 15. Reconstructed plan of Solomonic gate at Gezer.*

unravel the complexities of a site like Gezer, where buildings constructed mainly of stone require a sophistication of method in enabling walls to be dated which was far beyond the methods employed. Macalister's dating of the structures, and especially the defences, like that of his predecessors and his successors still for decades, was a matter of guesswork. Nothing emerged that could obviously be referred to Solomon's building operations.

The site, on low hills, is an elongated one. On the south side of the circuit is marked an excavation area with the annotation 'Maccabean Castle'. When Professor Yadin's excavations at Hazor had led him to compare his gateway with that of Stratum IV at Megiddo, he logically proceeded to wonder if a similar gateway could be identified in the third of the cities, in addition to Jerusalem, to which Solomon devoted the proceeds of the levy. From the plan of the so-called Maccabean Castle, he very convincingly disentangled the plan of a gateway with an inturn flanked by triple guardrooms, associated with a casemate wall (fig. 15).[34] The gateway includes the oblique approach with an outer, double-buttressed, gateway, virtually identical with that at Megiddo, though not required in connection with the lesser slope at Hazor. This interpretation of the Gezer evidence is completely convincing. At present, however, we lack any information concerning the rest of the defences and of the internal structures of Solomon's city.

At this stage in our evidence from excavations, it can be said that archaeology proves, as the actual evidence suggests, that Solomon introduced a new conception into the original tribal organisation of the Israelites. David had begun the revolution by making his capital in Jerusalem, captured by himself and with no tribal connections. But his expansionist and warlike activities had allowed him no time to develop his capital. This was undertaken by his heir, Solomon, who added to the Jebusite-Davidic city an extension which was essentially a royal quarter, for the Temple to provide (a revolutionary concept) a permanent home for Yahweh, and Solomon's adjacent Palace. Linked with this by the Biblical text[35] is Solomon's work at Hazor, Megiddo and Gezer. At Hazor it looks as if he established a real royal quarter or citadel. At Megiddo it is clear that his defences enclosed at least some official buildings, but it would appear that domestic quarters were enclosed by his defences. At Gezer there is no evidence. The general conclusion is that Solomon began the process of creating royal quarters, utterly alien to the long-persisting and democratic organisation of the Israelite tribes. The full development, however, comes in the subsequent period, that

[34] *I.E.J.* 8, p. 84, fig. 3.
[35] I Kings 9. 15.

of the Divided Monarchy, and especially in the Northern Kingdom of Israel.

There were certainly other large and important cities in Solomon's kingdom, notably Beth-shan and Lachish. At Lachish, excavation on the summit of the mound has not reached the Solomonic level, though it is possible that an imposing palace or residence[36] dates back to his time. At Beth-shan, the summit of the mound was occupied by two temples,[37] Canaanite in origin, but of which the continuance in use during the 10th–9th centuries[38] is one of the anomalies in the kingdom in which the worship of Yahweh should have been the sole religion; the existence of such anomalies appears in the Bible as an undertone, in the recurrent denunciations of the prophets of the back-slidings of the rulers and their people. But even though these sites may have had important public buildings, they cannot claim the distinctive title of Royal Cities, for they are not mentioned in association with Jerusalem as the object of Solomon's levy, as were Megiddo, Hazor and Gezer.

Not enough is known of the contemporary lay-out of Beth-shan and Lachish to enable any conclusions to be reached. But there is enough evidence from a number of smaller sites, for instance T. Beit Mersim and Beth-shemesh, to show what the ordinary run of Palestinian towns were like. The only recognisable public structures are their walls, inherited from a long history as local centres required to defend their lands during the Canaanite period. The domestic architecture is completely undistinguished, little cramped houses, irregularly planned, built of rough stones with no use of ashlar. Here in fact is the Palestinian vernacular architecture, continuing from the Canaanite into the Israelite period. Solomon lavished none of his wealth on the lesser towns and villages; indeed, they were probably impoverished by his taxation to build his Temple and Palace in Jerusalem and his Royal Cities. As will be seen, moreover, once the architects and masons of Solomon in Jerusalem and Omri-Ahab in Samaria had departed, the relapse into the vernacular building methods was rapid. The Israelites, in effect, had no skill as masons.

---

[36] *L III*, pp. 78–86.
[37] *Beth-shan, Four Temples*, pp. 22–35.
[38] *The Iron Age at Beth-shan*, especially pp. 138–9.

# 7 🌿 THE ROYAL CITIES OF THE DIVIDED MONARCHIES: SAMARIA

In 925 B.C. the United Monarchy of David and Solomon fell apart after a mere eighty years of existence. The immediate stated cause of the disruption was religious, the conflict of the orthodox with the heterodox. The basic reason was that the union was a personal one, dependent on the leadership of David and his son. Under them the southern and the northern group of tribes had been brought together. But with a weaker ruler, the separate history of the two groups, for long divided by the alien enclave of Jerusalem and with different histories of entry into Palestine, pulled the tribes apart again. The ten northern tribes became the Kingdom of Israel, the two southern tribes the Kingdom of Judah.

The Kingdom of Judah had one supreme advantage. To it belonged Jerusalem, though situated very near to its northern boundary. There was the fixed sanctuary of the symbol of Yahweh, the Ark. With this, nothing in the break-away northern kingdom could compete. Apart from this, Judah was certainly the poorer relation. The hostility of Israel to the north was almost continuous. To the west were the Philistine towns, backed by Egypt, to the south the desert areas leading to the Sinai peninsula, to the east the kingdoms of Edom, Moab and Ammon. Judah was in a strait-jacket, and archaeology shows that its culture was likewise circumscribed.

The position of the Kingdom of Israel was very different As one moves north, the physical configuration becomes less harsh. The summit of the crest broadens, not into a plateau but into more gentle valleys, rich in the terms of agriculture. Between this area and the Phoenician coast and inland Syria there is easy contact. The Kingdom of Judah was cut off from the rest of the western Asiatic world by the hostility of Israel, but Israel was wide open to all the influences of the contemporary cultures.

A capital had to be found for the northern kingdom. The first king, Jeroboam, established himself at Shechem, where he had been elected. But after a few years he abandoned Shechem and moved to Penuel in Transjordan, probably because the Pharaoh Shishak I was devastating the country. When Jeroboam returned, he established himself not, for some reason, at Shechem but at Tirzah. Here the capital was to remain some forty years. It was at Tirzah that Omri started his reign in 878 B.C. after he had usurped the power of Zimri. Up to that point, the ruling house in Israel had been as transient as the capital, but the house of Omri was to rule for some thirty years, and Omri was to provide Israel with a permanent capital at Samaria.

The situation of Tirzah remained uncertain until comparatively recently. It was proved to be at Tell el Farʿah by a nice combination of archaeological evidence. In the excavations at Samaria between 1931 and 1935[1] it was possible to distinguish six structural phases in the Israelite period, and to identify the pottery connected with each. Tell el Farʿah was excavated between 1946 and 1960.[2] The Iron Age levels show a break, and structurally an abrupt break, exactly at that point that Samaria was founded. From that point it was virtually abandoned for three-quarters of a century. This evidence seems conclusive. When Omri moved his capital, he must have taken the inhabitants of Tirzah with him.

Tell el Farʿah lies in the Wadi Farʿah, some 6 miles northeast of Shechem. It was a site of great antiquity, and obviously of considerable importance in the Early and Middle Bronze Ages. The Wadi Farʿah is one of the main tributaries of the Jordan, with water running the year round. The gradients of the valley are easy, and it therefore formed an important access from the Jordan valley and the east to the central ridge, in fact the only really easy route south of the Plain of Esdraelon. The town was situated in rich agricultural lands. But the site was not one suited to be the capital of the new kingdom. Its outlook was to the east and, situated well below the central crest, it turned its back on the west and north.

Omri's policy shows that he was more interested in the wider area of the more advanced culture of Phoenicia and Syria than in the hinterland of the east. The Biblical record says[3] that he reigned in Tirzah six years and that for the final six years of his reign he transferred the capital to Samaria. In a way that is quite unusual, archaeology confirms the story. The stage at Tell el Farʿah that precedes the period of abandon-

[1] S.S. 1–3.
[2] Interim reports R.B. LIV, LV, LVI, LVIII, LIX, LXII, LXIV. LXVIII, LXIX.
[3] I Kings 16. 23–24.

Pl. 38. The hill of Samaria from the
south-east.

ment ends with an unfinished building.[4] Omri had started to
build his capital and then became dissatisfied with it. The
Biblical record says[5] 'And he bought the hill Samaria of
Shemer for two talents of silver, and built on the hill, and
called the name of the city which he built, after the name of
Shemer, owner of the hill, Samaria'. Excavations have confirmed that he built on a virgin site. There had been some
occupation on the hill in the late 4th millennium,[6] but from
then on there were no buildings until those of the period of
Omri.

In transferring his capital, Omri must have had two things
in mind. The first would be the situation. The hill of Samaria
(pl. 38) is not high in relation to the hills to the north, east
and south, but it is well isolated from them, and to the west
a broad valley runs down to the Mediterranean. Today, the
main road along the central ridge, having passed through
the gap between Mount Gerizim and Mount Ebal, commanded by Shechem, curves round its western foot. It is highly
probable that the earlier main line of communications followed the same line, but even if it were further to the east, it
would still be commanded by the hill of Samaria. Samaria
therefore was assured of its contacts with Phoenicia and, via
the Plain of Esdraelon, with Syria. It must be remembered
that Omri's son was married to the Phoenician princess
Jezebel. It has been suggested[7] that in fact Omri was a
foreigner and not a Hebrew, which would be an additional

[4] R.B. LXII, pp. 582–3.
[5] I Kings 16. 24.
[6] SS 3, pp. 91–94.
[7] Noth, p. 230.

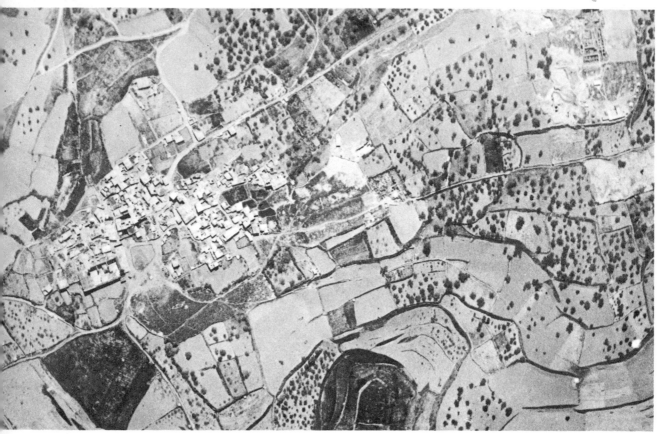

*Pl. 39. Air view of summit of hill of Samaria.*

reason for his interest in the outside world. To the west the site commanded the lowlands, limited only by the varying strength of Philistia; to the east were the fertile upland valleys, which had been part of the strength of Tell el Far'ah, but which were equally accessible from Samaria. It was an ideal situation.

The second consideration that must have been in Omri's mind was a new conception of a Royal City, a conception which, as will be shown, he developed elsewhere. This was that of a royal quarter. The Canaanite towns to which the Israelites fell heirs show very little social differentiation on the available archaeological evidence. There is no evidence that David constructed any royal palace or enclave in Jerusalem, though the remains are so scanty that this is not conclusive. Solomon probably, as discussed above (p. 42), constructed his Palace, like the Temple, as an adjunct to the existing town. Omri's revolutionary conception was a royal quarter dominating the centre of the city. For such a conception, he was at Tirzah restricted by existing buildings. A virgin site offered the ideal conditions, though at Megiddo a pre-existing lay-

*Pl. 40. Oblique air view of summit of hill of Samaria.*

*Fig. 16. Section across the summit of the hill of Samaria.*

out was adapted to this conception. To the end of the kingdom of Israel, this idea of royal supremacy and exclusiveness was unpalatable to the purists, as represented by the prophets.

The site Omri bought from Shemer was a gentle hill in comparison with Jerusalem. Nevertheless, the flat area of its summit did not provide a space adequate for Omri's conception of his palace. From the beginning, the buildings on the summit stood on terraces supported by retaining walls. Fig. 16, a section across the summit some 66 m. from its western end, shows how the early buildings were adjusted to the slope of the rock. On pls. 39 and 40, the area of the terrace shows up as the summit platform still defined by modern terraces.

SAMARIA
SECTION ACROSS SUMMIT
ISRAELITE LEVELS   PERIODS I AND II

A  STRATIFICATION NOT KNOWN  ROCK MINIMUM ORIGINAL HEIGHT  HEIGHT ABOVE SEA LEVEL B 435
430  SURVIVING FILLING OF PERIOD I  425

5 0 5 10 15
METRES

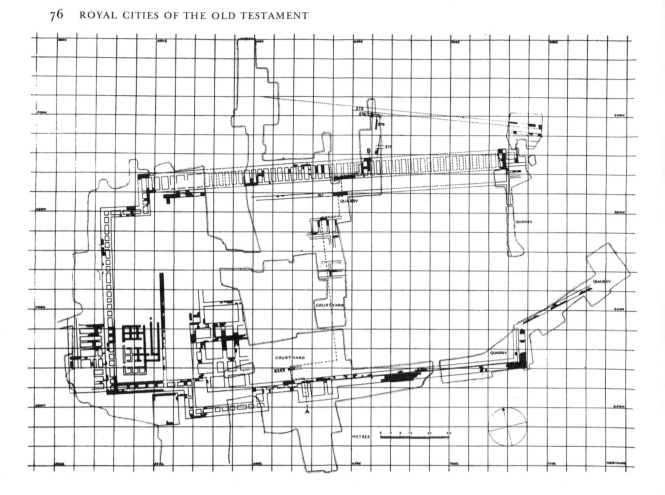

*Fig. 17. Plan of the Omri-Ahab buildings at Samaria.*

Omri's conception of his royal quarter was a terrace 145 m. from east to west and 76 m. from north to south, at the higher, western, end of the hill, open to the cool Mediterranean breezes. To carry out his conception, he called in Phoenician craftsmen. For Solomon's use of these foreigners, we have literary evidence, but no archaeological evidence has survived. For Ahab's use of Phoenician masons, the evidence is purely archaeological. The construction of the terrace supporting the royal quarter was in two stages. The earliest supporting wall was in a style of masonry dressing which was not equalled in Palestine, or indeed anywhere else in the Near East, until the time of Herod the Great in the 1st century B.C. The super-structure of the walls was of stones exquisitely dressed to a flat surface (pls. 41 and 42). The jointing of the stones was meticulous. If a corner was chipped, an exactly squared patch was inserted (pl. 43). The wall was a supreme example of the mason's craft. The foundations of this type of wall were of rougher stones, but with a very characteristic finish, in which

*Pl. 41. Samaria Period I wall of royal quarter.*

*Pl. 42. Samaria Period I wall of royal quarter.*

a fairly rough boss was left surrounded by two or three dressed margins, the upper margin usually being the broader. Stones of this type were also employed in the outer walls, those of the main defences or gateways (pls. 44 and 45). J. W. Crowfoot has shown[8] that this type of masonry is certainly

*Pl. 43. Meticulous patching in masonry of Samaria Period I.*

*Pl. 44. Bossed masonry of outer walls of Samaria Period I.*

*Pl. 45. Bossed masonry of outer walls of Samaria Period I; on left, tower of Hellenistic period.*

Phoenician, with its origins, on the evidence of Ugarit, in the 13th century B.C.

This conclusion is important not only for the appearance of Samaria, but also for Solomon's buildings at Jerusalem. On the Biblical evidence, Solomon had employed Phoenician craftsmen. One can conclude that the walls of his buildings were in the tradition of those, some eighty years later, that Omri's masons built at Samaria. One can therefore visualise the walls of the Temple as built in the exquisite flat-dressed masonry shown in pl. 42, and the retaining walls of the Temple platform built in the massive and idiosyncratic style shown in pl. 44. No fragment of the superstructure of the Temple will ever be found, but it is conceivable, if massive excavations to the depth of 80 ft. or more were to be undertaken round the circuit of the present Haram esh-Sherif, that the typical Phoenician bossed stones would be found at the base. The only archaeological evidence is that in the excavations on the eastern crest south of the Haram (site SII on fig. 9), a wall was found (pl. 27), in which bossed stones of the Samaria type were found. The wall was relatively late, with an 8th-century B.C. fill against it, and the stones were certainly re-used. But they provide evidence that there had been a wall using such stones in the neighbourhood.

[8] *SS 1*, pp. 5–9.

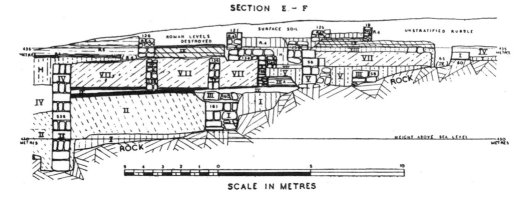

*Fig. 18. Samaria section showing face of original wall buried by the fill (II) inserted with the casemates.*

Omri's original enclosure wall of the summit area was perhaps symbolic rather than defensive, for the outer face is in finely dressed masonry (pls. 41 and 42). The face of this wall was buried to at least 2 m. in the second stage (fig. 18). The wall is shown as 161 in squares 450–460 N. in fig. 17, and the west side within squares 450–440 E. The original conception is therefore that of a separated royal quarter, rather than an acropolis, which is a character that it may rapidly have acquired in the second period. The remains within this enclosure wall are unfortunately fragmentary in the extreme. The only structures that safely belong to the original period are those shown on fig. 17 in the square 450–390 N., 630–650 E. Those in squares 510–590 E., 410–350 N. are certainly later, built in the rough indigenous style which is described below (p. 90).

The walls of the structures traced in this very limited area are foundational only, and many could be traced only by robber trenches. These were only located by the 1931–5 excavations, for at the time of the 1908–10 excavations archaeological technique had not reached the stage at which walls could be traced by the trenches from which they had been robbed. Even in the strip excavated right across the summit the robber trenches could only be identified in part, since west of c. 630 m. E. even the surfaces belonging to the earliest buildings had been destroyed by later structures. What survives suggests that the buildings were on a considerable scale. The foundations consist of massive stones a metre in length, laid as headers occupying the full width of the trench. Such stones are on the same scale as those employed in the enclosure wall, and laid in the same way. The fragments of the building, shown in squares 630–650 m. E., 410–450 m. N., suggest that it was spacious and well planned, and set back from the enclosure wall. To its south was a large courtyard, floored with hard-pounded lime plaster. Near the southern side of the enclosure was another building, of which only a very small fragment could be traced. One should probably visualise this royal quarter as containing a number of buildings, a larger one probably for the palace, possibly to the western end, more open to the western breezes, and a few other buildings for administrative purposes and perhaps the living quarters of the king's entourage. The excavations show that these buildings were set in wide courtyards. The conception is one very alien to the crowded, close-packed buildings of earlier Palestinian towns.

Omri ruled only six years at Samaria. He was succeeded by his son Ahab, famous in the Biblical story for two things—his wife Jezebel notable for her adherence to the cult of Baal,[9] whose prophets were dramatically defeated by Elijah on Mount Carmel[10] and for her fate,[11] and for the episode of Naboth's vineyard.[12] The fact of the association of the house of Omri with Tyre and the Phoenicians has already been mentioned as making it probable that Omri would turn to the Phoenician world to construct a capital of the type and style strange to Palestine. Ahab's 'ivory house' is discussed below.

Since Omri's rule in Samaria was so short, it is very reasonable to expect that Ahab's buildings were a direct continuation of those of his father's. There was certainly a very direct continuation, for on the limited grounds of archaeological dating by pottery, Periods I and II at Samaria cannot be distinguished. Stratigraphically they can be very clearly distinguished, and functionally the distinction is very important on sociological grounds.

Stratigraphically, the distinction between Period I and II is absolute. The beautifully faced wall of Period I (pl. 42) is buried to a depth of at least 2 m. by a fill retained by an outer enclosure wall, which thus added a rather narrow extension to the summit terraces. It is inconceivable that the fine face of the Period I wall was built with the idea that it would be foundational; the structural division between the two periods is certain, even though the rather wide limits of dating by the associated pottery cannot distinguish between them. The new enclosure wall is on the casemate plan, a double wall with cross-walls connecting an outer and inner wall. This was a form of town wall that, on a site in which levels were sloping up from the exterior, could present to the attacker the combined width of the outer wall, the inner wall, and a solid filling between, a great economy in stones and in labour as against a solid masonry wall of the equivalent width, and almost as effective. It was a method of construction certainly as early as the 10th century B.C.[13] and its use by Solomon at Hazor and Megiddo has already been described. At the interior

[9] I Kings 16. 31–36.
[10] I Kings 18. 19–40.
[11] II Kings 9. 33–34.
[12] I Kings 21. 1–16.
[13] Tell Beit Mersim Strata B and A, *A.A.S.O.R.* XVII, pl. 47

ground level, the spaces enclosed by the casemates were probably in all cases functional rooms. The plan of the Period II casemate wall of the royal quarter is shown on fig. 17. On fig. 18, illustrating its relation to the Period I wall, only the inner wall of the casemates is shown. On the north side, the casemate wall, running closely parallel to the original north wall, was 6·50 m. to its north and, up to the outer wall, added an effective width of 14·50 m. to the original summit terrace. To the west, where the casemates were shorter in depth but wider in width, the space between them and the original wall was 24 m. On the south side the new wall was ✔ simply added against the original wall, and for the most part there was no real extension. To the east, the position is uncertain.

Omri's original royal quarter was thus now surrounded by a massive enclosure wall. From the archaeological evidence, this took place without any long interval, and it is suggested that this development belongs to the time of his son Ahab. Certainly, from such evidence as survives for the original structures, it belongs to the time when the Phoenician building methods were still employed. But sociologically and administratively, the new structures are evidence of an important change. Omri's original conception was in itself revolutionary against the tribal background of Israelite society. A royal quarter, with the summit area separated from the rest of the town by an enclosure wall, within which were royal buildings spaciously situated in open courtyards, was an enormous divergence from previous traditions. In Period II, a still more important stage is seen. The royal quarter is surrounded by a defensive wall. The royal quarter has become an acropolis. The defensive wall surrounding this summit area was maintained, with at intervals extensive repairs, until the end of the kingdom of Israel, and it is significant that its lines were followed by the acropolis wall of the Hellenistic period.[14]

Excavation has in fact so far failed to reveal at Samaria the lower town that one would expect to exist to house the ordinary inhabitants outside the royal quarter. Excavations in 1968 by Dr. J. B. Hennessy, at the north-west of the summit area (the bottom right corner of pl. 40), showed that there was no occupation prior to the Persian-Hellenistic period. Further search is required in the area to the east, but for the moment we are left with the impression that the capital was administrative only, and that the inhabitants of Samaria carried away into exile by the Assyrians came from the surrounding countryside, taking refuge in the town in time of war. The same explanation is possible at Megiddo, (see p. 101).   [14] *SS* 1. pp. 118–20 and pl. IV.

The Biblical record is concerned with Ahab's wickedness, with his adherence to the cult of Baal in which his Phoenician wife Jezebel played a great part, and with his successful military operations. His great enemy was the prophet Elijah, who caused 840 of Jezebel's priests of Baal to be slaughtered on Mount Carmel,[15] and who bitterly condemned the murder of Naboth arranged by Jezebel to satisfy Ahab's desire for Naboth's vineyard.[16] 'But there was none like unto Ahab, which did sell himself to work wickedness in the sight of the Lord, whom Jezebel his wife stirred up. And he did very abominably in following idols, according to all things as did the Amorites, whom the Lord cast out before the children of Israel.'[17]

Ahab was a flagrant apostate from the religion of Yahweh. He succumbed (though with qualms in the face of Elijah's denunciations) to the pressure of the Canaanite culture that surrounded Israel. But in temporal terms he was a successful king. He reigned for twenty-five years, which in itself is evidence of his power. He twice defeated the might of Syria, led by Benhadad of Damascus,[18] though eventually he was killed in a subsequent encounter.[19]

The picture of Ahab that emerges is that of a reasonably successful ruler of one among a number of competing powers, none of them at that stage predominant, in western Asia. Just for this reason, he was anathema to the adherents of the pure religion of Yahweh. The risk was that the northern kingdom of Israel should be assimilated into the culture of the adjacent Semitic states in which the pantheon centred on Baal was the basic religion.

It is perhaps in this context that the obituary of Ahab mentions his house of ivory. 'Now the rest of the acts of Ahab, and all that he did, and the ivory house which he made, and all the cities that he built, are they not written in the book of the chronicles of the kings of Israel.'[20]

The mention is brief, without any explanation. A 'house' built completely of ivory would have been beyond the riches of Solomon or far more opulent oriental rulers. Clearly, however, ivory had in Ahab's palace a very prominent place. The clue to the interpretation came in the 1931–5 excavations. In the debris on the north side of the royal quarter was found a deposit of ivories.[21] The majority of the fragments were found in the debris of the Assyrian destruction of 722 B.C., many of them burnt black in the fire of that destruction. Some must have still been in use at that period. But enough fragments were in Period II deposits to show that they had belonged originally to the time of Ahab. They were terribly

Pl. 46. Ivory carving from Samaria.

[15] I Kings 18. 18–40.
[16] I Kings 21. 1–24.
[17] I Kings 21. 25–26.
[18] I Kings 20.
[19] I Kings 22. 1–38.
[20] I Kings 22. 39.
[21] SS 2.

*Pls. 47–51. Ivory carvings from Samaria.*

Pl. 47.

Pl. 48.

Pl. 49.

Pl. 50.

Pl. 51.

*Pls. 52–55. Ivory carvings from Arslan Tash.*

*Pl. 52.*

*Pl. 54.*

*Pl. 53.*

*Pl. 55.*

22 *SS* 2.
23 Barnett, *Nimrud Ivories.*
24 *Megiddo Ivories.*
25 *Arslan Tash.*

fragmentary and fragile, but enough survived to indicate their function and their artistic character. They were ornaments on a small scale suitable for adorning furniture, or perhaps occasionally as freezes on a wall. Ahab's 'house' was therefore not built of ivory, but lavishly decorated with ivory. The impression made by this decoration must have been such that Ahab's abode remained in the mind of the chroniclers as a 'house of ivory'. Not only was it spectacular, but it was exotic.

When these finds were first studied by Mr. and Mrs. Crowfoot,[22] there was not much comparative material. Objects carved in ivory were known on the Mediterranean coast from the Late Bronze Age onwards, notably in Cyprus[23] and, in Palestine, at Megiddo.[24] It was an art, or craft, with a relatively international spread, but with a centre on the Phoenician coast. The closest parallel to the Samaria finds, indeed very close in comparable objects and in dating, came from Arslan Tash in Syria, some 100 miles N.E. of Aleppo,[25] neatly dated to the period of Benhadad of Damascus, Ahab's adversary, for long defeated; ultimately, however, the might of Syria was responsible for Ahab's death. Many of the Arslan Tash ivories are very close to those of Samaria, though on the whole the Samaria ivories are finer.

However, the real picture of the craft of the artists in ivory of western Asia did not emerge until the excavations of Professor Sir Max Mallowan at Nimrud in Assyria. Nimrud is to be identified as the capital of the Assyrian kings from the time of Assur-nasir-pal, 884–859 B.C. to the end of the kingdom of Assyria in 614–612 B.C. From the year 740 B.C. onwards, the kings of Assyria pursued a steady policy of advance to the west. Megiddo and much of the northern part of the kingdom of Israel was lost in 733 B.C. and the capital Samaria fell in 720 B.C. after a siege lasting two years. In each of these forays, great quantities of loot were carried back to Assyria. The finds

Pls. 56 and 57. Ivory-decorated bedsteads from Nimrud.

*Pls. 58–60. Ivory carvings from Nimrud.*

*Pl. 59.*

at Nimrud provide an epitome of art history of the conquered lands of the Mediterranean coast, mingled with objects of art perhaps locally commissioned.

It could well be that the furnishings of Ahab's palace could not vie with those of the richer kingdoms to the north. But even if Ahab's palace at Samaria was equipped on a simple scale, the ivory-decorated bedsteads found at Nimrud[26] give an indication of how a ruler, intent on maintaining his standing among his contemporaries, would equip his palace (pls. 56 and 57).

The conclusions[27] of the study of the Samaria finds by Mr. and Mrs. Crowfoot was that the art represented by the ivories was Phoenician, and that Phoenician art was eclectic. This is supported by all subsequent evidence, and was very clearly illustrated by the Samaria finds. Pl. 46[28] looks to the non-specialist pure Egyptian, yet to the Egyptologist it looks alien. The lions of pl. 49 are at home neither in Egypt nor Meso-potamia. The lotus patterns of pl. 51 have an Egyptian flavour,

[26] *Nimrud*, II, pp. 411–15.
[27] *SS* 2, pp. 49–53.
[28] *SS* 2, pl. I. i.

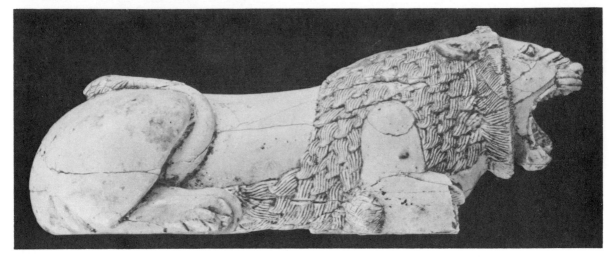

but are not Egyptian. From the very first studies, therefore, the finds from Samaria indicated that the artistic influence in the earlier years of the Israelite capital at Samaria were those of the cosmopolitan area of Phoenicia to the north.

The Nimrud excavations between 1949 and 1963 have now added enormously to the comparative material. Nimrud (Tell el Cal'ah) was the capital of Sargon II, who captured and destroyed Samaria in 722–721 B.C. In the storerooms of the palace at Nimrud were found enormous quantities of ivories. They could well include loot from Samaria; pl. 46 from Samaria and pl. 58 from Nimrud show how close the resemblances are. But the quality and the range of styles show, as is to be expected, that the ivories came from many sources. Many may have been loot from the various Assyrian campaigns in Syria and Phoenicia. Professor Mallowan, however, believes that some were made to the order of the Assyrian rulers and showed distinctive Assyrian styles.[29] All would, however, draw on the same cultural, artistic and technological tradition that was centred on Syria and Phoenicia.

It is perhaps the Phoenician element that the finds at Samaria especially illustrate. Throughout history, the Phoenician city states can barely be said to have a culture of their own. Their inhabitants were entrepreneurs, traders and essentially cosmopolitan. They passed on the commercial products of their own country (especially timber) and of the hinterland to Egypt, and from Egypt they passed Egyptian products on to the mainland of western Asia. Their artists and craftsmen derived inspiration from these international contacts. Ahab brought in these artists and craftsmen to decorate his 'house of ivory', and the international flavour of their products is well illustrated by the miserable remnants of the ivories found at

*Pl. 61. Ivory carving from Nimrud.*

[29] *Nimrud*, I, pp. 134, 144; II, p. 471 ff.

*Pl. 62. Ivory carving from Nimrud.*

Samaria. This evidence is vital to the understanding of the culture imposed by the house of Omri on the capital of the kingdom of Israel. The dividing line of Israel from its Semitic neighbours was small indeed.

The second contribution of the Nimrud finds to the interpretations of the ivories of Samaria is the clear evidence of their function. The great majority of the Samaria finds were plaques, either in low relief or *ajouré*. Only very occasionally were there carvings in the round, for instance pl. 49.[30] The plaques must have been affixed to something, and their small scale suggests that this was to furniture. The Nimrud finds make it clear that whole sections of furniture decorated with carvings in ivory were stacked in the storerooms. Pl. 56[31] shows the carvings attached to the head of a bedstead. This is the interpretation that one must put on most of the ivory finds at Samaria. The exuberance in the use of ivory in the furnishings is likely to be why Ahab's palace was described as a 'house of ivory'. It is reasonable to think that this same criterion can be applied to Solomon's throne.[32] A complete throne made of ivory, constructed even out of the most enormous elephant tusks, would have required exceedingly elaborate jointing, and it is reasonable to conclude that the ivory was a veneer.

The archaeological evidence allows one to deduce these points concerning the capital of the Northern Kingdom, the kingdom of Israel, during Ahab's time. The king was an autocrat, living in a royal quarter, which had ample room for his entourage, and to which Ahab added defences that converted it into an acropolis. The culture of the capital was cosmopolitan-Phoenician, and in religion that of the Israelites struggled, mainly unsuccessfully, with that of surrounding countries.

Reference has already been made to a further very important point that can be deduced from the Samaria of the Omri-Ahab period. On archaeological evidence we have a royal quarter built by Phoenician masons and its houses decorated by Phoenician craftsmen. This is just what the literary evidence describes in the case of Solomon's Jerusalem, eighty years earlier. The Samaria evidence and that with which it can be related can illustrate the literary descriptions of the decoration of the Temple. As is suggested on p. 48, the cherubim that guarded the Holy of Holies, with a wing span of 10 cubits[33] (5 m.), can be imagined from the Nimrud ivories, for instance pl. 23,[34] though these figures are only 8·2 cm. high. Decorative elements on the scale of those of Solomon's Temple no doubt existed elsewhere, but it is hardly surprising that they have not survived. We must be content and convinced by the small-scale surviving evidence of contemporary art.

[30] *SS* 2, pl. IX. 1.
[31] *Nimrud*, II, p. 491, no. 385.
[32] I Kings 10. 18.
[33] I Kings 6. 24.
[34] *Nimrud*, II, p. 549, no. 482.

# 8 ✤ THE LATER HISTORY OF THE ROYAL CITIES OF THE NORTHERN KINGDOM, ISRAEL

This study is concentrated primarily on the elements that comprise a Royal City. It moved from the original Royal City of Jerusalem to Solomon's other Royal Cities. In the interpretation or comprehension of much of this, the Samaria evidence has been invoked. Beyond the period of Solomon, the evidence, both literary and archaeological, fails us for the royal elements in Jerusalem. The subsequent history of Jerusalem as a town will be described below, but it adds little to the history of Jerusalem as a Royal City. It is probably a fair conclusion that after the division into the Southern Kingdom of Judah and the Northern Kingdom of Israel c. 930 B.C., the Southern Kingdom, poorly endowed with natural resources and surrounded by alien powers on every side, was, in modern terms, frozen. Developments came only in the Northern Kingdom of Israel. The history of the northern Royal Cities is therefore here treated first.

At Samaria, the structural evidence and the stratigraphical evidence from pottery established a very close connection between Periods I and II. Period III is markedly different on both counts. The pottery is distinct, and the structural evidence marks a distinct break. New buildings are added, and the style of the masonry, with roughly coursed blocks, is a complete break from the Phoenician-style masonry of Periods I–II. It is very reasonable to ascribe this break to the abolition of the Omri dynasty by Jehu in 841 B.C.

In the original lay-out, the internal buildings had been widely spaced in courtyards and set back from the surrounding wall. In Period III, large courtyards still existed, but, as shown

*Pl. 63. Period III wall at Samaria built on top of a Period I wall.*

*Fig. 19. Plan of Samaria Period IV buildings on the summit.*

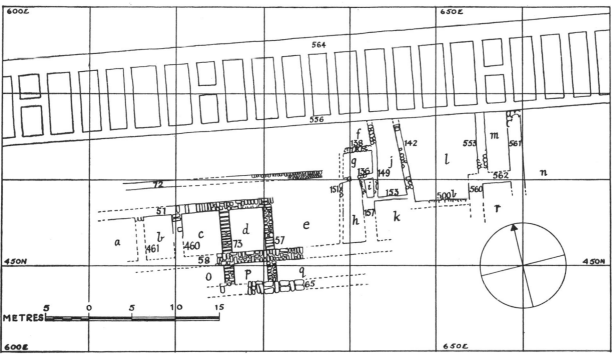

in the area where the stratigraphical sequence was best established, a process was begun of adding rooms to the north of the main building, which in Period IV culminated in the elimination of the original building and in rather shoddy and irregularly planned rooms being built up against the casemate wall as an addition to the Period III buildings. The difference can be seen in a comparison of fig. 17, where the Period I buildings are shown[1], and fig. 19, showing the Period IV buildings. Already in Period III, the finely built enclosure wall of Period I, which had been apparently left as an inner wall when the casemates were built, had been eliminated. Pl. 63, which shows a Period III wall built on the top of this wall, is an eloquent illustration of the complete disappearance of fine masonry.

[1] An exception is the building in 360–410 m. N., 560–600 m. E., of which the coarser style is evident even from the plan alone.

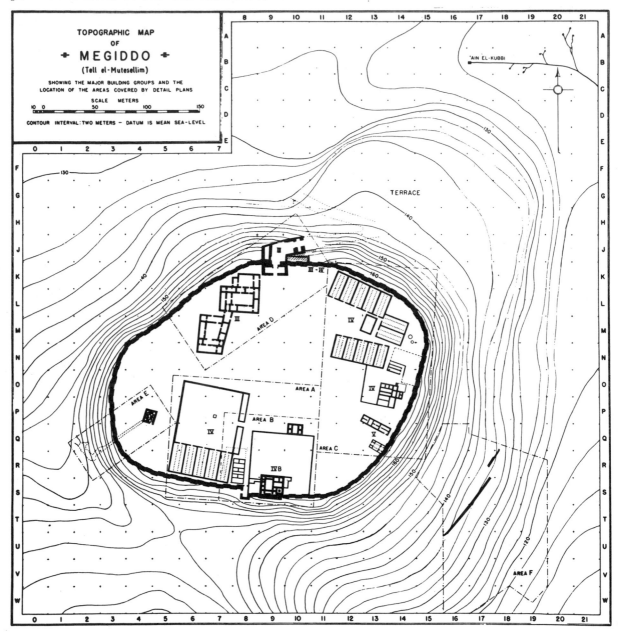

Fig. 20. Plan of Megiddo, mainly Period IV.

For the dating of the later periods of Israelite Samaria, there is not the historical evidence that dates Period I to c. 880 B.C.[2] Altogether, six stratigraphical stages are bracketed between that date and the Assyrian destruction in 722 B.C. The pottery evidence suggests that Period III is not separated by a long gap from Periods I–II.[3] A date of c. 840 B.C. would fit very well, and as already said, the break with Phoenician-style masonry is likely to belong to the time of Jehu (841–813 B.C.).

[2] The dates adopted in SS 1–3. Noth accepts a date for the beginning of Omri's reign of 878–877, and the foundation of Samaria would therefore be 872 B.C.

[3] SS 3, pp. 198–9.

Period IV, to which we shall return later, may date from c. 800 B.C.

The pottery evidence associated with these closely bracketed periods at Samaria is of considerable importance in establishing the history of Megiddo. The excavators of Megiddo uncovered in their Stratum IV a number of buildings of clearly public character; an overall picture is given in fig. 20, though it is now clear that the wall and gate shown thereon are later. The most striking component of these buildings is three sets of stables, one on the south side with a spacious attached courtyard and two in the north-east sector. These stables the excavators ascribed to Solomon. This ascription was tempting, for Solomon had 'cities for his chariots and cities for his horsemen'.[4] It is not precisely said that one of these cities was Megiddo, but this mention follows only four verses after the reference to Solomon's activities in his Royal Cities, so the location of one of his chariot cities at Megiddo is tempting. Doubt on this ascription has been frequently expressed. Doubt on the grounds that elements in the masonry are related to that at Samaria[5] is not perhaps as cogent as has been claimed, for the related derivation of Solomonic and Omrid architecture from Phoenician sources could account for resemblances. There are, however, four lines of reasoning that confirm the dissociation of the stables from Solomon's building operations. Firstly, the 'northern fortress' discovery by Yadin[6] was superseded by the northernmost stables; its association with the casemate wall which can with great probability be ascribed to Solomon is quite clear. Secondly, the administrative building 1482 adjacent to the 'palace' 1723, and clearly associated with it in origin both in alignment and orientation, was truncated by the great stable 1576 and its compound; here we have clear proof that the stables were not part of Solomon's original lay-out. Thirdly, it can be shown that the masonry associated with the stables and the other Stratum IV buildings is based on a re-use of stones derived from Solomonic structures, perhaps from the parts of the administrative building 1482 which were eliminated when the impinging stables were built,[7] and from the 'northern palace'; the greater part of the stones from the walls thereof were found to have been removed.[8] The masonry and the style of wall construction are described below, but it certainly is far from the Samaria standards, which can be deduced as having been comparable with Solomonic standards. Fourthly, the pottery evidence is quite conclusive. Some of the evidence would point to an even later date, but this may be because of intrusions not recognised by the excavators. The most conservative estimate suggests that the construction of the public buildings of Megiddo Stratum IV approaches the date of Samaria Period III.

[4] I Kings 9. 19.
[5] J. W. Crowfoot in *P.E.Q.* 1940.
[6] See p. 58.
[7] Kenyon, *Megiddo, Hazor, Samaria and Chronology, p. 149.*
[8] *I.E.J.* 16, p. 279.

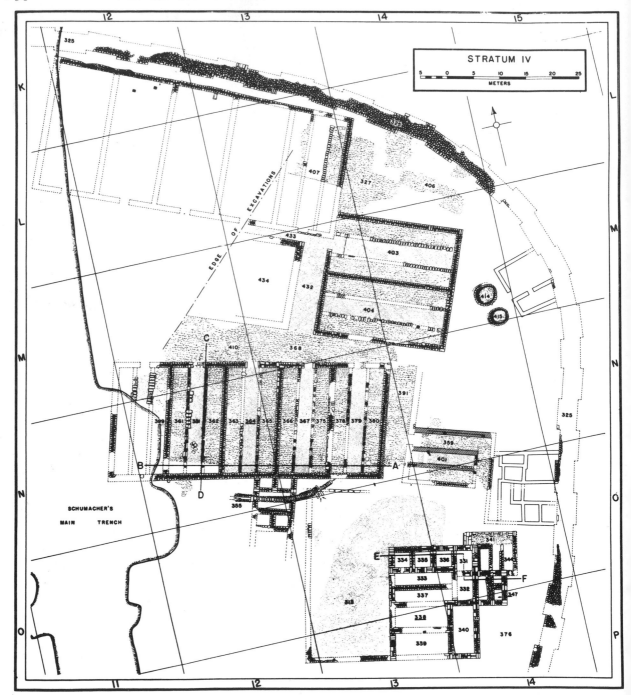

Fig. 21. Plan of Megiddo stables and building 338.

*Pl. 64. The south-east corner of building 338 at Megiddo.*

The clearest pottery evidence came from building 338, which is seen on fig. 21 with three of the lesser stable blocks. This building was set in a courtyard floored with lime-mortar surrounded by an enclosure wall, though this was largely destroyed. The pottery evidence is clear[9] that the date of this building approaches that of the time when the Samaria Period III building was constructed, that is to say c. 840 B.C. The building methods seen in pl. 64 are peculiar, and they are indeed very peculiar, to the excavators' Stratum IV. The greater part of the walls are of rough rubble, roughly coursed. At the corners and at intervals in the walls are piers of ashlars, bonding in with the rubble. The piers in the walls have usually a stretcher, then in the next course a header, and then a stretcher. The revealing point about these piers is that the different type of dressing of the ashlar blocks is used quite indiscriminately. The Samaria evidence makes it quite clear that the fine, flat-dressed ashlar blocks were used in the super-structure of fine buildings, the blocks with well-dressed margins and irregular bosses in foundations or in the super-structure of more rugged buildings such as town walls. They were never used together in the same course. Building 338, which can be taken as a key since its stratigraphical evidence seems precise, provides clear evidence that in the Stratum IV structures these canons were ignored. Pl. 64 shows with great clarity that the greater part of the superstructure of the south-east angle (though there can be doubts about the second course) is built of fine ashlar, flatly dressed, yet the piers to the

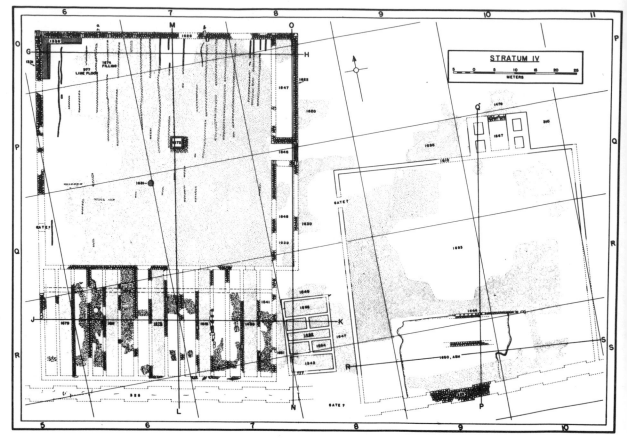

*Fig. 22. Plan of Megiddo stables 1576 and courtyard of 'palace' 1723.*

north-east, certainly, and to the north-west, probably, as seen in pl. 64, show very clearly that in the courses corresponding with those at the angle in which there were these fine ashlar blocks, there were these different types of ashlar blocks in adjacent piers, and *M I*, fig. 65 shows that one of the fine ashlars at the corner was broken before it was re-used. These instances in which the use of ashlar blocks at Megiddo does not appear to conform with the originally planned use of the blocks can be multiplied.[10] The conclusion is that those structures that employed this peculiar use of ashlars belongs not to the period when this type of treatment of stonework was introduced into Palestine by, as has been shown, Phoenician masons, but to a period when the skill of the Phoenician masons was no longer available, though when buildings belonging to the period of these masons could be a source of building material.

This 'pier' type of wall-construction is in fact typical of the greater part of the excavators' Stratum IV lay-out, the great compound of stable 1576 (fig. 22), the enclosure wall and the other stables.

[10] Kenyon, *Megiddo, Hazor, Samaria and Chronology*, pp. 149-50.

*Pl. 65. Stable unit 351 at Megiddo.*

The stables are very interesting structures. They consist of long compartments with a triple division. The central one, c. 3 m. wide, was approached by a wide doorway (pl. 65), and the discovery of a number of stones with a cavetto at one end suggested to the excavators that these stones supported the lintel and helped to span the width of the opening. The central gangway was ordinarily floored with lime-mortar. It was divided from the two side units, again 3 m. wide, and floored with cobbles, by stone piers (pls. 65 and 66). In the piers were tethering holes. Between the piers were stone troughs or mangers (pl. 67, visible also in pl. 66). Each of these pier-manger units, c. 1·67 m. wide, presumably represents one stall. A curious feature is that the mangers, c. 0·70 m. high, form with the intervening piers a continuous division between the gangway and the stall area. The exception is in the division next to the entrance, where no mangers were found. It would seem, therefore, that the horses could be only led out by whole units; access to an individual horse at the far end was impossible. This suggests a very military approach; horses moved by troops, not as individual animals, but one would feel that

every now and then, in case of illness or wildness among the horses, that must have been an inconvenience.

The southern stables (fig. 22) are distinguished from those in the north-east sector by having associated with them a large compound, 55 m. square. The construction of these stables involved the truncation of the administrative building 1482 (compare this building in figs. 12 and 22). The alignment of the stables and the compound is at an angle to that of the 'palace' 1723 and its enclosure, which is an additional reason for ascribing them to a different period. The only certain entrance into the stable compound was on the east side. It was flanked by two compartments c. 4 m. deep which together extended the whole north–south length of the compound. The excavators suggest that those were 'garages' for chariots,[11] separated from the compound area by an open arcade; the suggestion is plausible, but there is no evidence. The creation of the courtyard was a considerable constructional problem. The slope down of the preceding structure had been from the south-east to the north-west. The eventual slope to the north

*Pl. 66. Stable 364 at Megiddo.*

[11] *M I*, p. 35.

Pl. 67. Manger in stable 364 at Megiddo.

of the lime-mortar floor of the compound was only slight, 2 m. in 55 m.[12] Yet the difference between the foundation level of the walls at the south-east corner of the stables and the north-west corner of the compound[13] (the foundation level is of course not an absolute indication of floor level, but is suggestive of the relative strength of the walls) is of the impressive order of 7 m. This does not imply that the terracing-up for the stable compound was anything like 7 m., but it shows that there was a great depth of fill at the northern side of the compound, which had to be supported by enclosure walls with substantial foundations. A section through the centre of the compound[14] shows the depth of fill against the north wall as 4 m., compared with 1 m. at the south side; the depth against the south-west corner was said to be greater.

The compound was clearly an artificial platform, constructed to provide an approximately level surface over a previously sloping area. To achieve this, a fill of very great proportions had to be imported. It is suggested by the excavators[15] that this was derived from a clearance from the approach to the water

[12] M I, p. 34.
[13] M I, p. 32.
[14] M I, fig. 35, section L–M.
[15] M I, p. 32.

shaft which was adjacent; as will be shown, it is more likely to
have been from the original excavation of the shaft. Structurally, the compound imposed on the engineer-architects the
problem of a great fill of unconsolidated material, supported
by enclosure walls. To reduce the effect of soil shift, the
engineer-architects introduced a succession of strainer or
compartment walls, which are seen on fig. 22 and pl. 68. They
are very clearly non-structural, and their purpose was to
control the shift of the fill that made up the platform of the
compound. In spite of these precautions, there was uneven
settling of the fill, over which the surface of lime plaster
which floored the compound and ran through into the gang-
ways in the stable had at intervals to be renewed.[16] There is a
strong presumption that these repairs, the contents of which
would certainly have been ignored in the primitive stratigraphical technique employed, introduced into the fill beneath
the floor the pottery that suggests a later date than that of
other buildings with which on structural grounds the stables
and their compound are to be associated.[17]

Approximately in the centre of the courtyard was a sunken
rectangular tank constructed of mud bricks, with an internal
plastering of mud mortar. The tank was approximately 2·30 m.
square and 2 m. deep. Its contents when full would have been
c. 10·58 cu. m. or 2,775 U.S. gallons.[18] A curious feature is
that there was no obvious supply of water to this tank. There
was not even any system of drains channelling off into it the
surface water from the compound. It must have been filled
by man- (or more probably woman-) power from the nearby
water shaft. It is reasonable to suppose that the normal
procedure would have been to take the horses down to the
plain at the foot of the mound to water at a spring.[19] The tank
may have been a provision for times of war, when this was not
possible.

The evidence of the pillars and mangers in the lay-out of
the stables was sufficiently clear to enable the excavators to
calculate the numbers of horses that could have been housed.
There was a change of plan in the southern stables, with an
extension to the north to accommodate an extra thirty horses.[20]
The ultimate scheme would seem to provide for 450 horses.[21]
The excavators adduce evidence to suggest that in Palestine
and Syria, more hilly than Egypt, the normal complement of
horses to a chariot was three.[22] The structures at Megiddo as so
far excavated would therefore provide for a complement of
150 chariots, perhaps, on the evidence of the way the stable
units are broken up, divided into three squadrons of fifty
chariots and 150 horses.

[16] *M I*, pp. 33–34.
[17] Kenyon, *Megiddo, Hazor, Samaria and Chronology*, p. 150.
[18] *M I*, p. 34.
[19] *M I*, p. 35.
[20] *M I*, p. 44.
[21] *M I*, p. 43.
[22] *M I*, p. 44.

*Pl. 68. Strainer wall in make-up of courtyard of southern stables at Megiddo.*

The lay-out of Megiddo at this stage is of explicit centralisation. There is evidence that a great part of the summit of the mound is occupied by official structures and the strong presumption is that the whole of the summit came within the same lay-out. Domestic dwellings were expelled to the lower slopes, about which we know nothing; Megiddo may have become a purely Royal City or there may have been domestic occupation on the slopes—exploration to investigate this has a considerable sociological interest. Recent investigation, however, does not suggest that an area that was probably a lower town was in fact occupied at this period,[23] so here, as at Samaria, we have no evidence for anything except a royal quarter. The summit plan incorporates part of Solomon's tentative development of a Royal City. The southern 'palace' 1723 remains in existence, and its extensive courtyard is built or, more probably, rebuilt. The administrative building 1482 adjacent to it is truncated. The great further developments are the stables. Certainly associated with these great public works is some stage in the major construction of the means of approach to the water supply at the south-west angle of the mound.[24] The Solomonic approach to the spring has been already described (pp. 67–68). This was succeeded by a

[23] Verbal communication from Professor Yadin.
[24] See *M I*, fig. 3 (or revised fig. 23).

much more ambitious approach which could belong to this stage, though there is so far no conclusive evidence. It cannot indeed be later, for alterations can be dated to the 8th century, and since its predecessor, the gallery, is now known to be Solomonic (see pp. 67–68) it seems to fit as part of the major constructions of this phase. It consisted of a vertical shaft 35 m. deep, with at its base a horizontal tunnel 63 m. long (fig. 23). The upper part of the shaft (pl. 69) was cut through the accumulated deposits of the mound and was revetted in masonry, and the lower part was cut deeply into the rock. The tunnel was of course entirely rock-cut (pl. 70). The whole undertaking indicates astonishing engineering skill, with the depth of the shaft to the level of the spring and the direction of the tunnel towards the spring calculated with only very small errors. At a time when no compasses, theodolites, or other scientific instruments to measure direction and levels

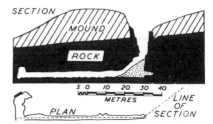

*Fig. 23. Plan and section of Megiddo water shaft.*

*Pl. 69. Looking down the shaft to the water tunnel at Megiddo.*

were available, it is a most remarkable achievement. It also indicates a very considerable control of man-power, for to hew a way for this depth and distance through solid rock, and to carry out and dispose of the resultant debris, was a colossal undertaking, worthy of the architects and engineers of a Royal City. A further point is worth making. This approach to a water source was calmly and scientifically planned. It is very different from the way in which the Siloam tunnel at Jerusalem, certainly considerably later, was executed, for this bears all the evidence of a frenetic haste in the face of hostile threat (see pp. 137–140). The Megiddo water system was part of a planned development of a city.

It remains to consider who was responsible for this second phase of Megiddo as a Royal City. The first phase certainly belongs to the period of the United Monarchy of Israel. The second equally certainly belongs to the period when the

*Pl. 70. Tunnel to spring at base of water shaft.*

unified kingdom had fallen apart into the southern Kingdom of Judah and the northern Kingdom of Israel. Megiddo of Stratum IV, as just described, was part of the northern kingdom, with its capital at Samaria. The Omrid dynasty fell heir to Solomon's Royal Cities of Megiddo and Hazor. The available evidence links the most securely dated structures of the new layout with Period III at Samaria[25] for which a tentative association with the disruption of the Phoenician contacts by the expulsion of the Omrid dynasty suggests a date of c. 840 B.C. The construction of Samaria Period III is associated with an identifiable range of pottery forms, new as compared with those associated with the construction of Period II, ascribed (see p. 81) to Ahab. But unless there is a catastrophic destruction of a civilisation, the appearance of new pottery forms is a gradual process. The vessels associated with Samaria III did not appear at the moment that Jehu (if the interpretation of the structural evidence is correct) started to rebuild Samaria in the indigenous, rough techniques, because he no longer wished to use the foreign, Phoenician, masons. The pottery forms had been evolving throughout Ahab's reign of twenty-five years. The best dated structures of Megiddo Stratum IV, building 338,[26] shows that some of the vessels that can be dated by parallels from Samaria have associations with Samaria Period III. My own view is that the ascription of some of the Megiddo Stratum IV structures, on the evidence of pottery from the associated fill suggesting a date in the 8th century B.C.[27] is due to inadequate excavation technique. My view of the evidence upon which one must base one's interpretation of the clearly public lay-out of Megiddo IV, is that its date is ± 840 B.C. Therefore it either belongs to the period of Ahab or to that of his successor, Jehu. Both were powerful kings. Ahab reigned for twenty-five years, Jehu for twenty-eight. The immediately apparent aim of the lay-out of Megiddo was to provide for horses and chariots. Jehu's reputation in connection with chariots appears in his descent on Jezreel to seize the kingdom from Ahab's son Joram, for the watchman reported 'and the driving is like the driving of Jehu the son of Nimshi; for he driveth furiously'.[28] Ahab's army of chariots was by far the largest contingent in the combined forces of the small states of Syria and Palestine that, at the battle of Karkar in the valley of the Orontes in northern Syria in the year 853 B.C., tried to oppose the relentless advance to the west of the Assyrians. According to the records of Shalmaneser III,[29] Ahab's contribution to the combined force was 2,000 chariots and 10,000 soldiers. Most records of this sort give exaggerated figures, for the king and his scribes wished to suggest the great

[25] *SS 3*, p. 202.
[26] *Ibid.*, p. 202.
[27] *Ibid.*, pp. 202–3.
[28] II Kings 9. 20.
[29] Gressman, *Altorientalische Texte und Bilde zum Alten Testament*, 2nd edition, 1926–7, p. 340 f.

strength of the opposition over which victory was claimed. The Assyrians claimed the battle of Karkar as a victory, but in fact it must have been inconclusive, for after it the *status quo* remained, and it was followed by no immediate surge forward of Assyrian power.[30]

The records may give exaggerated numbers, but they show Ahab as a powerful ruler amongst the Syro-Palestinian states, and they emphasize that he had at his command a very considerable chariot force, a form of armament important when warfare in the plains of Syria was contemplated, though less suited to the hilly country of Palestine itself. Anyone who felt impelled to maintain a substantial band of chariots must have had his eyes on a wider field than that of the area controlled by the ruler of the Northern Kingdom of Israel, much of which was barely suited to chariots.

In contrast with Ahab, Jehu did not attempt to intervene in the Syrian area to oppose the subsequent thrusts of Shalmaneser III. He apparently offered no military opposition, and the Black Obelisk of Shalmaneser records his tribute.[31] Though Jehu was, as has been said, a powerful king, the Israel of his time was apparently no longer an international power.

From this historical evidence, there seem clear grounds for ascribing the Stratum IV lay-out of Megiddo to the time of Ahab. On the basis of the Samaria pottery evidence, a date in the 850s B.C. would be perfectly suitable. A base such as the Royal City of Megiddo of Stratum IV would be very suitable for the launching in 853 B.C. of the great expedition of '2,000 chariots and 10,000 soldiers' for the battle of Karkar. Ahab's reign of twenty-five years was long enough for the Phoenician masons responsible for the early buildings to have gone home, and for the recrudescence of local, rougher building methods.

The evidence for the secondary stage of a Royal City is much more dramatic than is available, on the present incomplete state of our knowledge, for the first stage. It was only at Megiddo that a relatively large area was involved and there were great modifications when the Royal City of a United Monarchy became a Royal City of a separate northern kingdom.

Of the Royal Cities, Hazor was the companion of Megiddo in being transferred to the control of the Northern Kingdom. The evidence is not yet available to assess any resultant developments, for the evidence from the buildings of the Solomonic level is not yet fully published. The pottery evidence suggests[32] that the building of the Hazor IX stage is contemporary with that of Period II at Samaria, the modification of

[30] *Noth,* p. 246.
[31] Gressman, *op. cit.* See also *Noth,* p. 247.
[32] Kenyon, *Megiddo, Hazor, Samaria and Chronology,* p. 148.

the original lay-out that is ascribed to Ahab. In this period, the casemate wall of the royal quarter continued in use without any change.[33] The excavators were confident that a stage in what they call the pillared building, clearly a public building on any interpretation, belongs to this period, though the fullest evidence of its structure is assigned to Hazor VIII. The description[34] is not completely clear; Stratum IX is said to be marked by a strongly defined burnt level. It seems probable that this is meant as defining the end of Stratum IX, and on the assessment of stratification and pottery proposed,[35] this could represent a destruction when Jehu drove out the Omrid dynasty. But any uncertainties concerning the detailed events are irrelevant for a general picture of the successive stages of Royal Cities. The evidence from Hazor is clear that the defences of a royal quarter, or acropolis, established in the time of Solomon, with the associated royal or official buildings, continued into the next period of the divided monarchies. This next stage is very probably to be ascribed to Ahab.

Stratum VIII at Hazor was probably built at about the same time as the Period III buildings at Samaria,[36] that is to say at about the time that Jehu drove out the Omrid dynasty in 841 B.C. The evidence certainly suggests that there were very considerable changes affecting the royal quarter at Hazor, for apparently the casemate wall that had enclosed it was abolished, and for a period there was no substitute.[37] Though no evidence to the effect has been clearly published, it must surely be expected that there was a wall lower down the slope encircling the whole town, and it is probably to be deduced that a wall at the east end of the mound, in area G,[38] based on a Middle Bronze Age foundation[39] represents this lower area. But as far as the royal quarter is concerned, there were no independent fortifications. However, the official character of the area is confirmed by the fact that important public buildings had their origin at this period, or were continued from earlier periods; the excavation of the lower levels as so far published is not conclusive in this respect.

At the west end of the area originally enclosed by the casemate walls of the Solomonic period an imposing building 25 m. by 21·50 m., with outer walls c. 1·90 m. to 2 m. thick, is attributed in origin to Stratum VIII,[40] though its description has only been published in detail for Stratum V.[41] It is a reasonable supposition that this building of considerable defensive strength took the place of the defence wall that separated the royal quarter from the rest of the city. It was planned symmetrically with long corridors in the centre and flanking ranges of rooms. It seems clear that it was approached only by an outside flight of stairs (visible at the

[33] *H II*, p. 4.
[34] *H II*, pp. 4–5.
[35] Kenyon, *Megiddo, Hazor, Samaria and Chronology*, p. 148.
[36] Kenyon, *Megiddo, Hazor, Samaria and Chronology*, p. 148.
[37] *H II*, p. 44.
[38] *I.E.J.* 9, p. 88.
[39] *I.E.J.* 8, p. 8.
[40] *H III–IV*, pl. XXXI; *I.E.J.* 8, p. 4.
[41] *H II*, pp. 51–52.

*Pl. 71. Air view of citadel at Hazor.*

*Pl. 71. Air view of citadel at Hazor.*

right upper corner of the building in pl. 71) to an upper storey, with the lower parts of the building used only for storage.[42] This conception of a massive building structure on a podium, only entered at first-floor level, certainly adds to its official character. Adjacent to it were other buildings, some with earlier origins, which from scale could have had an administrative character, but the evidence is not so clear.

[42] *H II*, p. 52.

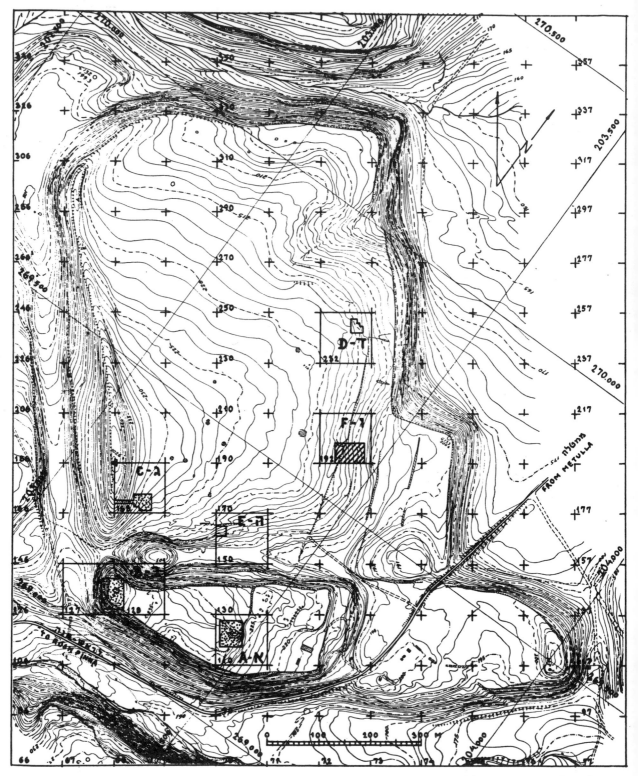

*Fig. 24. Contour plan of Hazor.*

*Pl. 72. Pillared building, probably a royal storehouse, at Hazor.*

In the other area excavated, Area A towards the eastern end of the area enclosed by the Solomonic walls (fig. 24), an imposing building, called the Pillared Building, certainly belongs in its fullest development to Stratum VIII. It consisted of a building 21 m. by 13·50 m., with the tripartite division, basilical in plan, formed by two rows of monolithic piers (pl. 72, see also in pl 29). There is an obvious superficial resemblance in the plan of the building to that of the Megiddo stables. The excavators are, however, clear that the resemblance is only superficial and that the building was a royal storehouse,[43] and that it should be interpreted in connection with the adjacent bipartite building to the north; their arguments seem convincing.

A recent addition to the public buildings of Megiddo to be attributed to Stratum VIII is a magnificent water shaft, closely resembling that of Megiddo. It lies on the north side of the mound, and may be expected to be aiming to reach the water supply in the valley to the north. It is a great rectangular shaft. The upper part is cut through the accumulation of earlier strata on the mound, including walls ascribed to the

[43] *H II*, p. 9.

Solomonic Stratum X. This upper part has surrounding revetting walls. The lower part is cut in the rock, and has rock-cut steps sloping down the side walls, just as at Megiddo. The base of the shaft has not yet (January 1969) been reached, so one cannot tell whether at its base a tunnel led successfully out to the water-supply, as at Megiddo. But it already has the same aspect of a grandiose piece of official engineering.[44]

At Hazor in the second half of the 9th century B.C., therefore, we seem to have the continuation of a summit-area occupied by official buildings, though it is no longer divided from the rest of the town by its own individual fortifications. The position is therefore different from that at Samaria, where the casemates of Period II certainly continued to divide the royal quarter from the rest of the town. The difference is perhaps due to the fact that Samaria was the abode of the monarchy.

For the third of the Royal Cities associated with Jerusalem in the Solomonic period, there is unfortunately no evidence at all. As has already been said, the early excavations at Gezer provided no stratigraphical evidence, and it is only the inspired hypothesis of Professor Yadin that has rescued the Solomonic gate from previous uncertainty. For the rest of the history of the Royal Cities, Gezer has to be left aside.

[44] I am indebted for a visit to this most interesting find to the courtesy of Professor Yadin. Details have subsequently been published in *I.E.J.* 19, pp. 12–19.

# 9 ✤ THE LATER HISTORY OF THE ROYAL CITIES

The later history of Jerusalem as derived from excavation is regrettably scanty. As already described (pp. 45–46), all structural and stratigraphical evidence on the summit of the ridge has disappeared through the combined effect of quarrying in Herodian and Roman times and, in most of the available area, of early excavations which would have destroyed any fragments of original evidence that might have survived the quarrying. On the eastern slope, which was not affected by the quarrying, almost everything except some small areas of the final stage, which will be described in the next chapter, has disappeared in erosion, caused by destruction of the supporting walls—destruction either due to enemy action or to natural causes such as earthquakes or torrential rain. The excavations have only provided some hints as to the history of the site, and the full implications will not be clear until the laborious business of correlating all the finds, especially the pottery, has been completed, a task requiring several years' work.

The area most historically productive for the time of the kingdom of Judah in the 1961–7 excavations was low on the eastern slope, above the Spring Gihon (see fig. 14). This was the area in which the original defences of the Jebusite-Davidic town were located (pp. 26–27). This original wall had a very long life. Only its lower part, foundational as regards the higher levels on the interior, survived, so it is impossible to establish to what extent the original Jebusite wall, dating to c. 1800 B.C., required rebuilding by David and his successors, or indeed during the later Jebusite period. Structural evidence of one rebuilding of the Israelite period survived (pl. 13), but it was not closely datable.

The main evidence for the continuance in use of the original wall is in the relatively late date of its successor. It was certainly upstanding during the 8th century B.C., for scattered traces of occupation at its foot, including an oven, must date to this period (pl. 73). Eventually it was buried by deposits running up to a successor, deposits that included a road running parallel to the line of the wall.

*Pl. 73. Outer face of Jebusite-Davidic town wall at Jerusalem with oven at its foot.*

It is to the periods that precede this successor that belongs the most interesting evidence secured by the 1961–7 excavations for the history of the central period of the Kingdom of Judah. The road associated with the immediate successor of the original wall (pl. 74), for it crosses the top of this wall and runs along the foot of a rock scarp, above which the later walls were built. Beneath the road are various structures. Some

*Pl. 74. Cobbled street over original town wall at Jerusalem.*

were in the nature of platforms or terraces, certainly belonging to a period when the original wall was still upstanding.[1] Almost certainly to the same period in which the original wall (which had disappeared to the north-west beneath the later wall (see pl. 75) was still functional belong some very remarkable structures. On present evidence, these are therefore extra-mural.

The first part of what may be a single complex was discovered in 1962, and more completely excavated in 1963–6.[2] The first element to be found was a shallow recess at the base of the rock scarp (already mentioned as that at the base of which the road runs) barely worthy of the name of cave. The most immediately striking point about this recess was that it was enclosed by very substantial walls (pl. 76), and that the gap between the walls and the rock was filled with mud plaster, pierced and re-plastered on a number of occasions. It looked at first sight as though the walls were intended to surround an entrance into a rock chamber, and the impression was somewhat similar to the shaft of a rock-cut tomb, such as those found at Jericho. The first finds fitted such an impression, for in the area between the walls and the rock was found a great quantity of pottery vessels, many of them complete (pl. 77). Such a deposit is very often found in the shaft of a tomb, being offerings placed with earlier burials and thrown out when later burials were made.[3] But this interpretation was soon disproved. The cave hardly extended beyond the area of the pottery deposit, and there was no evidence at all of human bones. Walls associated with those that enclosed the cave continued to the north, and it was clearly necessary to expand the excavated area, at the great labour of starting again from the top and digging through all the accumulated layers of wash.

*Pl. 75. In foreground, original town wall of Jerusalem, disappearing beneath later wall.*

[1] *P.E.Q.* 1968, p. 106.
[2] *P.E.Q.* 1963, p. 11; *P.E.Q.* 1964, pp. 8–10; *P.E.Q.* 1965, p. 6; *P.E.Q.* 1967, p. 66.
[3] E.g. *Jericho I,II, seriatim.*

Pl. 76. Cave in Jerusalem Square
A XXI, with surrounding walls.

Pl. 77. Deposit of pottery in cave
in A XXI.

The excavation of the extended area made it quite clear that we were dealing with a cult centre (pl. 78). Immediately to the north of the cave was a small room in which there were two standing stones. In such a small room they had no structural significance as roof supports, and they must be interpreted as cult stones *mazzeboth*. A *mazzebah* as a representation of the deity is well known in the Canaanite religion, and the worship of such is condemned by the prophets of Israel.[4] Nevertheless, the use of such stones certainly remained an Israelite practice. For instance, Absalom set up to himself a pillar as a memorial in his lifetime.[5] The room with the *mazzeboth* lay at the foot of the rock scarp in which the cave was cut. It was not built directly against the rock face, and between its west wall and the face of the scarp there was a distance of c. 30 cm. On the ledge on top of the scarp there was a small stone-built structure, c. 1·75 m. by 1·50 m., unconnected with any other walls. Its excavation revealed no diagnostic features. But what is quite clear is that it was much too small to have been a room. The only reasonable interpretation is that it was the base of an altar. To this interpretation a curious feature in the *mazzeboth* room can be taken as additional evidence. As has been said, the west wall was separated from the rock scarp by a distance of only c. 30 cm. Yet in this wall was a doorway (pl. 80). At a later stage, this was blocked, but it certainly formed part of the original plan. As a functional part of a building, it

*Pl. 78. Cave in A XXI, with associated* mazzeboth *and altar.*

[4] E.g. Jeremiah 2. 27.
[5] II Samuel 18. 18.

Pl. 79. *Altar on scarp, with narrow slot separating the* mazzeboth *room from the scarp.*

Pl. 80. Mazzeboth *room with blocked doorway in rear wall.*

makes no sense; one could lean through it but not walk through it. The only interpretation that can be suggested is that it enabled libations to be poured at the foot of the altar on the scarp above.

The interpretation that this evidence suggests is that in this extra-mural area there was a cult centre alien to the religion of Yahweh, at a spot only some 300 m. from the southern limits of the Temple compound. The function of the cave in this complex would be as a depository of vessels offered to a deity, which could not thereafter be used for profane purposes. Though until the time of Josiah in the second half of the 7th century B.C., there were other sanctuaries, many of them inherited from the Canaanites,[6] in which religious ceremonies had been carried out, nominally at least, in the worship of Yahweh, it is inconceivable that there should have been any shrine of Yahweh at Jerusalem other than in the Temple. It is, however, all too clear that there were places of heathen worship very close to Jerusalem. 'And Solomon did evil in the sight of the Lord, and went not fully after the Lord, as did David his father. Then did Solomon build an high place for Chemosh, the abomination of Moab, in the hill that is before Jerusalem, and for Molech, the abomination of the children of Ammon.'[7] These 'high-places', a generic name for a heathen sanctuary, apparently had a long life, for in the cleansing of Judah of heathen practices by Josiah, the 'high

[6] II Kings 23.8; *Noth*, p. 276.
[7] I Kings 11. 6–7.

Pl. 81. Scarp in Jerusalem Square A XXVI with entrance to cave and associated structures.

places that were before Jerusalem' were described as those built by Solomon, and to the earlier list is added one 'for Ashtoreth the abomination of the Zidonians'.[8] The extra-mural situation of the sanctuary just described would be entirely suitable for a centre of an unorthodox cult, tolerated by all except the priests and prophets of Yahweh, but not to the extent of inclusion within the walls of the Davidic or Solomonic city.

The structures connected with the claimed sanctuary have still not been completely excavated; they extend further both to the north and east. It is certain that nothing further would be recovered to the east, for other clearances have shown that the destruction slope would have cut through them just beyond the excavated area. To the north, allied structures, or the continuation of the same complex, may exist, but it was impossible to undertake a further major clearance from the surface.

To the south, however, a further find was made in the final season of excavation, certainly connected with the same or an adjacent sanctuary.[9] The same rock scarp as that in which the original cave was cut continued across the area (pl. 81). Along the edge of the scarp ran the road that was associated with the first successor of the Jebusite-Davidic wall (see p. 112). Beneath it was a building constructed against the scarp, and the central feature in this building was a well-cut entrance into a cave. This cave was a very different affair from the shallow scoop which was the introduction to the complex to the north. It was an approximately rectangular main chamber, c. 3·40 m. deep, 3·20 m. wide and c. 2 m. high, with well-cut and horizontal

[8] II Kings 23. 13.
[9] P.E.Q. 1968, pp. 108–9.

Pl. 82. Interior of cave in A XXVI after clearance.

floor and ceiling (pl. 82); to the rear were two bays 4·80 m. deep and 2 m. wide, and 1·60 m. deep and 1·5 m. wide, divided by a pillar of rock, leaving a communicating 'window' between them. The general plan of the cave, obviously completely man-made, would be perfectly suitable for a tomb of the period. It could be that this was its original use, but if so, not a trace survived. The sole use for which evidence did survive was as a tip (pl. 83), mainly of pottery vessels, many intact or possible to mend, but also many figurines, both

Pl. 83. Pottery tip in cave in A XXVI.

human and animal, and a considerable number of animal
bones. The pottery vessels consisted mostly of normal domestic
utensils, though four among them were interesting, but not
unique, in having graffiti inscribed on them, the significance of
which has not yet been worked out. One vessel of the domestic
type was outstanding as the largest cooking-pot ever found
(pl. 84). A pottery vessel certainly not of domestic use was a
magnificent incense stand (pl. 85), of a type known from cult
centres at Megiddo and Beth-shan. The human figurines are of
a type common elsewhere in the Jerusalem excavations and on
other sites, but interesting since they are so numerous, and
since they are so obviously representations of a fertility cult,
of the Mother Goddesses found over many centuries and many
lands in western Asia.

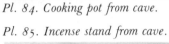

*Pl. 84. Cooking pot from cave.*

*Pl. 85. Incense stand from cave.*

The widespread distribution of such obviously heathen
objects provides a clear illustration of the reasons for the
denunciations of heathen practices by the prophets. The Palestinian Iron Age representations of the type are often known
as pillar figurines, for the base of the figure is pillar-shaped.
presumably representing a flowing robe sweeping to the
ground. In the torsos, the breasts are shown as magnificently
developed (pl. 86), often with the arms clasped beneath them;
it is rare for examples to be found with the head attached,
since these were obviously made in separate moulds. The
examples from the caves are only remarkable as compared
with many other specimens found during the excavations in
that they are better preserved. This is also true of the animal
figurines (pl. 87, 88, 89). Quite innumerable examples have
been found with portions of bodies and stumps of four legs or
of heads with a muzzle and two ears, which one can interpret
according to taste as a horse or a dog. The examples from the
cave were considerably more complete. In some, riders could
be attached to their mounts. In others, a reasonably identifiable horse had on its forehead a disk, a feature not so far
recognised elsewhere on the site. It is tempting to call this a
sun-disk, and to think of those as miniatures of 'the horses that
the kings of Judah had given to the sun', which Josiah took
away.[10]

As in the smaller, earlier-found, cave, most of the elements
in the finds could be paralleled in domestic circumstances.
But in domestic circumstances, one does not find complete
pottery vessels thrown away. This, quite apart from the strong
admixture of other elements such as the incense stand and the
numerous figurines, suggests again a cult association, a depository of dedicated gifts. The building complex does not
have the elements that can be interpreted as having cult significance that were found in the complex just to the north.

[10] II Kings 23. 11.

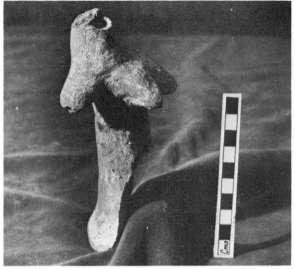

Pl. 86. Fertility figurine from cave.

Pl. 87. Horse with rider from cave.

Pl. 88. Horse with disk on forehead.

Pl. 89. Horse with disk on forehead.

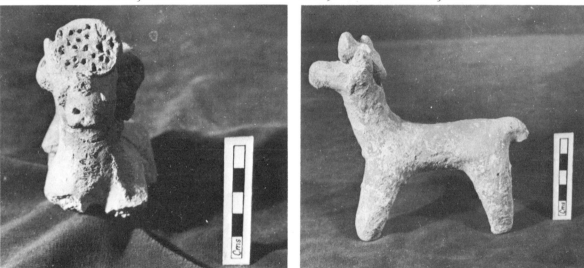

The neatly paved room seen in pl. 81 is unusual but clearly not diagnostic. Nevertheless, there is a strong presumption that this cave was a depository associated with a cult centre, either that to the north or an adjacent one. The existence of such heathen sanctuaries so close to the heart of Jerusalem gives a most revealing insight into the struggles of the followers of Yahweh against the followers of the ancient religions of the land

The dating of the use of the cult centre or centres is dependent on the assessment of the pottery evidence. Certainly, there

Pl. 90. First surviving wall to succeed the original east wall of Jerusalem.

is nothing in what has been found that goes back to the time of Solomon. The finds belong to a fairly late period in the life of the kingdom of Judah. It cannot be put too late, since, as will be seen, there are following this period a number of episodes in the rebuilding of the defences in this area that precede the final catastrophe of the Babylonian destruction at the beginning of the 6th century B.C. The assessment of pottery evidence is a laborious process. The finds from all deposits have to be examined and correlated, and when the site succession has been determined, it has to be compared with evidence from elsewhere. Until this process has been carried out, conclusions are only provisional. With these provisos, the present conclusion is that the date of the material from the cave is ± 700 B.C.

The great interest of the find of these structures is the factual evidence provided of the strength of the heathen cults, associated with the Canaanite pantheon with its strong emphasis on fertility rites, even at Jerusalem, the centre of the worship of Yahweh. There could be no more vivid illustrations of the denunciations, warnings and forebodings of the prophets.

The next stage in the history of Jerusalem, in this area low on the eastern slope where alone the evidence survives, is the building of a successor to the long-lived original wall. To this, reference has already been made. The evidence for it is entirely inferential. Above the Jebusite-Davidic wall was a succession of levels, culminating in a north–south road (pl. 74), which (especially the road) implies that they were supported to the east by a retaining wall; this it can certainly be assumed was a town wall. The road, and the underlying and overlying levels, are, moreover, quite certainly cut by the wall that visually succeeds the original one (pl. 90). In the fairly limited area in which excavations were carried east across the line that must have been followed by this presumed wall, not the slightest trace survived, for the angle of denudation cuts obliquely down to below what must have been its foundation level.

It is impossible, until all the evidence has been assessed, to date this vanished wall and to associate it with events historically recorded. It could well be that the fact that its foundations did not have the security of a base on bedrock (which is proved stratigraphically) indicates that it was built in haste at a time of peril and, since the evidence from the secondary and other structures associated with the levels that must precede it preclude an early date, it could be that this vanished wall belongs to the time of Hezekiah, when Jerusalem was in great peril from the Assyrians (see below, p. 135).

Either at the period of the vanished wall, or earlier, there was certainly an extension northwards of the occupation on the eastern slope. As has been shown, the Jebusite-Davidic town had its northern boundary as indicated in fig. 6 (pp. 29–31). The Solomonic extension was along the crest of the ridge (p. 43). The excavation of Square A XXIV (pl. 91) provided the crucial evidence. There is a very remarkable contrast with

*Pl. 91. Jerusalem Square A XXIV, with at base the earliest building in this area, 8th–7th century in date.*

the excavated area only 20 m. to the south. Instead of the complicated terrace structures with Late Bronze origins and Iron Age II reconstructions, a laborious excavation to bedrock (pl. 81) revealed only two periods, both Iron II, belonging to an advanced stage in the history of the Kingdom of Judah. The earliest buildings were of massive structure, rectilinear in plan, based on bedrock (pl. 91). It is absolutely certain that they belong to an extension to the north beyond the area supported by the Jebusite-Davidic-Solomonic terraces. The chronological assessment of this extension on the slopes of the hill is still dependent on the detailed analysis of the pottery. What can be said at present is that at a stage subsequent to the Solomonic extension north confined to the summit of the ridge (see fig. 9), there was an expansion along the eastern slopes to include a new quarter within the town. A first survey of the evidence suggests that this was late 8th/early 7th century B.C. This extension is a competitor for identification as the *Mishneh,* the 'second quarter', referred to in II Kings 22. 14, but it cannot be claimed that there is enough evidence to exclude other competitors.[11] It could be expected that it would go with the successor to the original wall, but it could also be that there was an extension directly onto the north-east corner of the original wall, an area not excavated; the probability can be better assessed when the pottery has been fully examined.

The next stage in the history of the defences on the eastern slope consists of a wall set back at least 5 m. to the west, of which a considerable portion survives. This must, in all its stages, belong to the final century of Jerusalem as a Royal City, and it is dealt with in the next chapter.

At Samaria, the capital city in the northern kingdom of Israel, the structures of Period III have been assigned to the period of Jehu, 841–813 B.C. (p. 90), with the evidence from them of a break with the Phoenician building methods and a reversion to the rougher indigenous methods. Period III is succeeded by the buildings of Period IV. The building methods were similar, but the associated pottery provides distinctive dating evidence.[12] The casemate wall of Period II, probably belonging to the time of Ahab (p. 81), was rebuilt[13] (pl. 92). The process of building more shoddy walls, now actually impinging on the free space against the enclosing casement wall (fig. 19), was continued. But it would seem that the main conception of the royal quarter remained the same, not only in the rebuilding of the enclosing casemate wall, but in the existence of a main courtyard in the centre of the strip excavated across the summit of the hill, for a re-surfacing of the courtyard runs up to the Period IV building.[14]

An interesting commentary on the functions of this summit

[11] See e.g. *Vincent, J de l'A.T.,* pp. 647–651; *Simons,* pp. 156, 290–2.
[12] *SS I,* p. 105.
[13] *SS I,* pp. 99, 103.
[14] *SS I,* p. 105.

*Pl. 92. The rebuilt casemate wall of the royal quarter at Samaria.*

area at Samaria as a royal quarter is provided by the Samaria ostraca found by the Harvard expedition[15] in a building in the summit area which from structure certainly did not belong to the original lay-out. The ostraca consist of memoranda written in ink on sherds from pottery vessels, mostly bowls, and an analysis of the sherds suggests that the latest belong to Period IV.[16] The probable interpretation of the memoranda is that they record deliveries to the king of produce due as taxes, and they are recorded under regnal years that are usually interpreted as the ninth, tenth, fifteenth and seventeenth years of the king. An alternative reading of the number[17] would provide shorter reigns as possible alternatives, but the more usual interpretation and the archaeological evidence would combine to assign the ostraca to the reign of Jeroboam II, 781–742 B.C., the latest of the four reigns of the length required for the usual interpretation of the numbers. From the point of view of an illustration of the function of this summit area at Samaria, the exact dating of the ostraca does not matter. The evidence of the pottery is that the ostraca belong to a date of ± 800 B.C. At that date, a record of tax receipts, and probably the produce represented by these taxes, was stored in a building in the royal quarter; this we can take as evidence of the continued use of the enclosure, for a royal residence and for the administrative buildings through which the king administered his kingdom.

An interesting expansion from the evidence of Samaria concerns the history of T. el Far'ah, the site identified as Tirzah, from which Omri transferred the capital of Israel (see p. 72). As has already been said (p. 73), there is an abrupt break at

[15] *Samaria, H.E.* I., pp. 227–46.
[16] *SS* 3. pp. 469–70.
[17] Yadin, 'Ancient Judean Weights', *Scripta Hierosolymitana* VIII.

T. el Far'ah, with a building stage left uncompleted.[18] The archaeological evidence for this break corresponds nicely with that for the archaeological evidence for the foundation of Samaria. Thereafter at T. el Far'ah there is a period of virtual abandonment. A slight amount of material indicates a beginning of re-occupation contemporary with Samaria Period III, assigned to the period of Jehu.[19] But the full re-emergence of the site as an important town in the excavators' Period II is certainly contemporary with Samaria Period IV. The correspondence between the finds at the two sites is close to the last detail. Tirzah at this stage was not a Royal City, but its culture was clearly closely bound up with that of the capital, and its expansion at this stage at the beginning of the 8th century B.C. can be taken as an example of urban development and prosperity. It is interesting that, in the lay-out of the town, there is evidence of a distinction between a quarter in which there were houses of the well-to-do and an adjacent quarter with much inferior houses,[20] a distinction which does not appear in the earlier levels down to c. 1000 B.C., and which is an illustration of the attacks of the prophets against such social differentiation.[21]

The evidence from Megiddo supports that of Samaria for the continuance of a royal quarter in the 8th century B.C. The most probable assessment is that all the great lay-out of official buildings and stables belongs to the mid 9th century (see pp. 93 ff). But some of the deposits claimed by the excavators to be associated with these structures must be assigned to the time of Samaria Period IV; this is especially the case in connection with the southern stable 1576 and its compound.[22] It seems inconceivable that this complex does not in origin belong to the main unitary lay-out of the royal quarter. The most probable interpretation is that there were intrusions not isolated by the summary stratigraphical techniques employed, and it is probable that much of this later material belongs to the repairs required in the compound to make good sinkages in the made-ground of the underlying fill (see p. 100). It can therefore be taken that the lay-out of the official buildings of Megiddo, here assigned to the mid 9th century B.C. and probably to the period of Ahab (p. 105), continued in use into the 8th century, contemporary with Samaria Period IV.

At some stage, there is a major alteration, consisting of the building of a new town wall, and involving the destruction of the 'palace' 1723, though leaving its courtyard intact. This wall is shown in the north-east sector[23] and in the southern area,[24] and it is clear that it encircled the summit. Professor Yadin has shown[25] that it is later than the casemate wall attributed to

[18] *R.B.* LXII, pp. 582–3.
[19] *R.B.* LXII, pp. 583–7.
[20] *R.B.* LIX, pp. 564–6.
[21] Amos 5. 11 ; Isaiah 9. 8–9.
[22] *SS 3,* pp. 202–3.
[23] *M I,* fig. 49, here fig. 20.
[24] *M I,* fig. 34.
[25] *B.A.* XXIII, pp. 62–68.

Solomon. The original excavations showed[26] that the offsets and insets wall involved the abolition of 'palace' 1723. There is no clear evidence so far for dating this wall. It cannot be ascribed to the full phase of Stratum III, for the 'palace' courtyard, to the surface of which it was joined by a floor over the robbed foundations of the 'palace' wall,[27] was abolished by the Stratum III buildings,[28] which will be referred to later, but it continued in use as the city wall of this stage. The Solomonic gateway apparently continued in use with the offsets and insets wall, which abuts against it (fig. 11), and it is possible that the secondary wall flanking the approach-way belongs to this stage, since it is similarly constructed. In origin the wall must belong to a modification of the royal quarter, presumably at a stage in which renewed defences were required, but at which the 'palace' administrative building was no longer necessary. If the deposits suggested above as being secondary to the main Stratum IV buildings can be·taken as dating the abolition of the 'palace' and the construction of the offsets and insets wall, it should date from early in the 8th century B.C. Apart from this,. the only evidence is that it must precede the destruction of Megiddo by the Assyrians in 732 B.C.

At Hazor, Stratum VII is probably contemporary with Period IV at Samaria, thus early 8th century B.C.[29] In it, official buildings continued to exist on the summit of the mound, without any acropolis defences. In particular, the pillared buildings at the north end of the summit area continued in existence,[30] with a new floor c. 0·50 m. above the original one. At the south end, the citadel ascribed in origin to Stratum VIII[31] continued in use, without any observed alterations.

In Stratum VI, which on correlation with Samaria should be mid 8th century B.C.,[32] the citadel continued in use, but at the north end of the mound occupied by the royal quarter, the changes were greater. The pillared building ascribed to Stratum VIII (see p. 109) was abolished, though the two-aisled building to its north continued in existence. The public character of the pillared building is rightly emphasised by the excavators.[33] The buildings that succeed it are on a considerable scale,[34] but their character, with small subdivisions and diverse plans, shows that they were private houses, shops and workshops.[35] This development is of considerable significançe. The royal quarter of Hazor had been deprived of its encircling defences in Stratum VIII, and now, perhaps a hundred years later, ordinary buildings encroach on the royal quarter. As far as present evidence goes, this was not the case at Samaria. It can be concluded that, in the outlying cities, monarchical control was diminishing.

The final stage of Israelite Hazor, Stratum, V, is represented

[26] M I, p. 97.
[27] M I, fig. 34 and fig. 35, section P–Q.
[28] M I, fig. 72.
[29] Kenyon, Megiddo, Hazor, Samaria and Chronology, p. 148.
[30] H II, p. 14.
[31] I.E.J. 8, p. 4.
[32] Kenyon, Megiddo, Hazor, Samaria and Chronology, p. 148.
[33] See p. 106 ff., H II, p. 9.
[34] H II, pl. CCII.
[35] H II, p. 19.

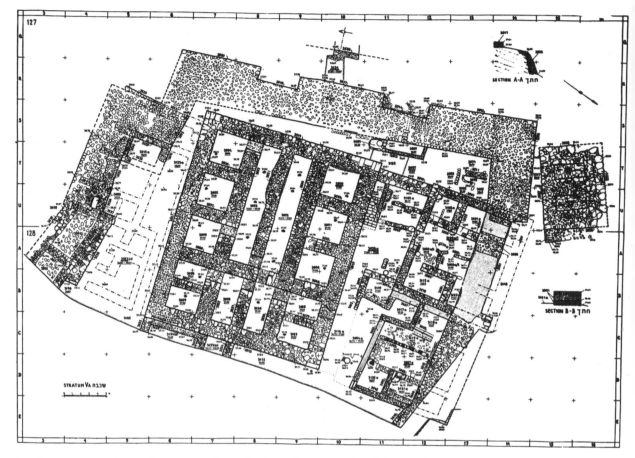

STRATUM Va שכבה

SECTION A-A חתך

SECTION B-B חתך

by the construction of a new wall enclosing the summit of the mound. Its plan at the west end of the mound enclosing the citadel, which still continued in use, is shown on fig. 25. It was built partly on top of the Solomonic casemate wall, using its limits, but inserting a solid filling into the casemate enclosures. The excavators have not yet traced the full extent of this new wall; it may have enclosed only the summit of the mound, the original royal quarter, but since it has not been found in the excavators' Area H at the east end of the mound,[36] it seems more likely that it enclosed a larger area. The planning of this new Stratum V wall is of interest. It is constructed with a series of recessed sections, and is therefore an offsets and insets wall, corresponding in plan with that which at Megiddo is an addition to the Stratum IV official building (pp. 126–7). This correlation in defensive methods fits very well the evidence of history. In the second half of the 8th century B.C., Megiddo and Hazor were facing the thrust of the advancing power of Assyria. Current military engineering suggested that the most efficient form of defence was that of this offsets and insets wall, with the possibility of enfilading the attackers, and at both sites are found defences on this plan.

*Fig. 25. Plan of citadel and wall of Hazor Stratum Va.*

[36] Cf. *H II*, pl. CCIII.

# 10 ❧ THE LAST YEARS OF THE MONARCHIES OF JUDAH AND ISRAEL

Megiddo and Hazor built new defences in the second half of the 8th century B.C.; the evidence from Samaria is not so precise, but it is to be expected that here too the signs of the times were recognised. After a period of quiescence, the existing major power of Mesopotamia, at this stage Assyria, was advancing to the west. Ahab had been concerned with warfare against Assyria; any local success against the threat from the east was transient, dependent mostly on internal politics in the Assyrian capitals. By the second half of the 8th century B.C., the pressure of Assyria on the minor kingdoms of Syria and Palestine had become overwhelming. In Palestine, the brunt of the first stage of the advances naturally fell first on the northern kingdom of Israel. The final crisis for Syria and Israel began with the accession to the throne of Assyria of Tiglath-pileser III in 745 B.C. Conquests to give him control of the Mediterranean coasts and of the rich timber and mineral areas that bordered it were one of his principal objectives. The age was over in which the kingdoms of Syria, Palestine and Transjordan, many of them in their turn relatively powerful, as for instance was the Israel of David and Solomon and the Syria of Benhadad II, could be considered to be of international importance. From now on great empires, initially from the east, based on Mesopotamia—Assyrian, Babylonian and Persian—and then from the west—Hellenistic and Roman—controlled the fate of the peoples of the Mediterranean coast.

Tiglath-pileser's advance into Syria began with his subjugation of Hamath in 738 B.C.; adjoining states up to the Phoenician coastal cities paid him resultant tribute. Menahem

of Israel, who·succeeded to the throne of Israel after complicated intrigues following the death of the last of the heirs of
Jehu,[1] took the same precaution.[2] The hopes of these tributaries that they would thereby escape from annexation were
vain. In 734 B.C., Tiglath-pileser made a great foray into
Philistia, the coastal area of Palestine, as far as the Egyptian
border. Complicated alliances and intrigues could not build
up any effective opposition against this vast power, and in
733 B.C. the greater part of the north of Israel was annexed to
Assyria and converted into Assyrian provinces, with the associated policy of transferring all the upper classes of the population to other parts of the Assyrian Empire.[3] The kingdom of
Israel was truncated, but its capital Samaria briefly survived.
Shalmaneser V succeeded Tiglath-pileser III. Each succession
of rulers in Assyria brought a brief respite to the threatened
states of the west, while the new ruler secured his position at
home. Shalmaneser began a siege of Samaria c. 724 B.C., and
it fell to his successor Sargon in 722–721 B.C. This was the end
of the Kingdom of Israel. Its area was incorporated in Assyrian
provinces, and its population deported and displaced by
groups forcibly transferred from other parts of the Assyrian
Empire. The deportees were no doubt basically the prosper-
ous urban peoples. The peasants were probably left. Nevertheless, the change in population was radical; from now on the
people of the southern kingdom of Judah despised the
'Samaritans' as of impure, mixed race.

The archaeological evidence of these events in the northern
kingdom is clear. At Megiddo, the Stratum IV buildings were
covered by a layer of destruction debris. The excavators
deduce a period of 'non-occupation' of two or three decades.[4]
This is possible, but the evidence for it is not clear. What is
quite clear is that there was a complete architectural break
between Stratum IV and III. The official buildings of the royal
quarter disappear. They are succeeded by a lay-out that is new
to Palestine. This is well seen in Area A on the south side of
the mound, which in Stratum IV had been occupied by the
'palace' 1723, with its courtyard 1693 and the stables 1576
with their compound (see fig. 20). It was thus one of the most
important areas of the royal quarter. In Stratum III the
change is dramatic. The whole area is covered by private
houses, laid out in a series of approximately rectangular insulae (fig. 26). All the other areas published show this same
lay-out in insulae. The inference is twofold. The summit of the
mound was no longer reserved for official buildings, and
secondly a new town-planning concept was introduced. Rectangular insulae of this type are alien to Iron Age Palestine.
They are an anticipation of Hellenistic-Roman town planning,

[1] II Kings 15. 10.
[2] II Kings 15. 19.
[3] II Kings 15. 29.
[4] *M I,* p. 62.

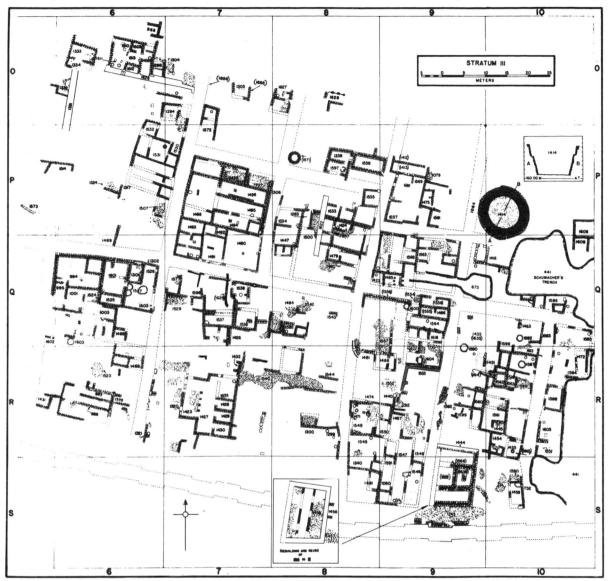

*Fig. 26. Plan of Megiddo Area A, Stratum III.*

but they have their parallels in the planning of Assyrian towns.

Both from the revolutionary change in the lay-out of Megiddo and from the pottery evidence, Stratum III can be seen to be the town established after the northern part of the Kingdom of Israel was annexed to the Assyrian Empire c. 733 B.C. Following on the destruction of the Israelite town, at an interval for the length of which there is no evidence, a completely new town was created. It was probably occupied largely by groups imported to take the place of the exiled urban population of Israel, but the changes of population were not absolute, for the basic culture, on the evidence of pottery and other finds, indicates continuity, though the only structural feature to link the two periods was the offsets and insets wall, which was certainly retained in use.

At Hazor, the citadel building at the south-west end of the mound had remained a dominating feature from Stratum VIII. In Stratum Va, it was enclosed by an offsets and insets wall (see p. 128), which obliterated parts of adjacent structures. In Stratum IV, the citadel was completely abolished.[5] The evidence from this area and from the eastern end of the mound[6] indicates that the successor to the final summit area defended by the offsets and insets wall was an open settlement, for no defences can be attributed to it. Hazor in the immediate period following the Assyrian conquest would appear to have been in an even worse state than Megiddo. There is no evidence that it was thereafter a place in which urban development was encouraged.

Megiddo and Hazor were the first of the Royal Cities of the northern kingdom to fall to Assyria. The fate of the capital city of Samaria, and of the rest of the Kingdom of Israel, was not long delayed. The king of Israel, Hoshea, was misguided enough to believe that the power of the Assyrians was at full stretch. He therefore withheld the tribute that he had promised as a result of Tiglath-pileser's conquest, and turned to Egypt for backing.[7] The reaction of Assyria was rapid. Shalmaneser V, who had succeeded Tiglath-pileser III in 727 B.C., first captured Hoshea, though on this we have no details.[8] 'Then the king of Assyria came up, throughout all the land, and went up to Samaria, and besieged it three years.[9] Samaria in fact survived this devastating siege sufficiently long to fall only in 722–721 B.C. to Shalmaneser's successor, Sargon III, a tribute to its defences even if only a small part of the Assyrian forces was employed against it. The catastrophic result of the capture of Samaria is recorded both in the Biblical record and archaeologically.

The Biblical record[10] says '. . . the Lord removed Israel out of his sight, as he had said by all the servants his prophets. So Israel was carried out of their own land to Assyria unto this day.' These are the ten lost tribes who reappear in so many cranky theories. 'And the king of Assyria brought men from Babylon, and from Cuthah, and from Ava, and from Hamath, and from Sepharvaim, and placed them in the cities of Samaria instead of the children of Israel: and they possessed Samaria and dwelt in the cities thereof.' This policy of wholesale transference of populations was basic to Assyrian policy; the Assyrians did not obliterate the populations of conquered countries and leave the areas derelict, for this would have been

[5] *H II*, pp. 52–53, 58.
[6] *H II*, pp. 43 and 58.
[7] II Kings 17.4.
[8] *Ibid.*
[9] II Kings 17. 5.
[10] Kings 17. 23–24.

uneconomic. But by breaking up all indigenous cohesion, they reduced enormously the chances of opposition to their policy. The disorientated new settlers would be relatively pliant to the wishes of their masters.

The archaeological record is equally eloquent of the complete destruction of the capital city. Though something of the spaciousness and elegance of the lay-out of the royal quarter of Omri and Ahab had been lost in the intervening century and a half, and the standard of building had greatly deteriorated, the royal quarter itself had remained emphatically in existence. The enclosing casemate was in fact extensively repaired in Period IV.[11] In Period V, there were fairly considerable alterations to the buildings adjoining the northern casemates;[12] these are ascribed to the mid 8th century B.C. At a slightly later date, Period IV, there was a rebuilding 573 of the middle terrace wall (see fig. 17) which probably flanked a road curving round the north side of the summit of the royal quarter to provide a route into the city from the west gate.[13] This wall, which may be regarded as an intermediate defensive wall, is probably the last structure which can be associated with Israelite Samaria, though it is just possible that it was built by Sargon at such an early stage after the capture that only pottery of the final Israelite period was lying about to be included in the contemporary fill.[14] My own inclination is to regard it as a final stage in Israelite building.

Elements in this middle terrace wall survived to be incorporated in defences of the Hellenistic period.[15] But the whole of the structures of the summit royal quarter perished completely at the end of Period V–VI. Fig. 18 shows the rooms of the final Israelite buildings filled with Period VII debris, much of it burnt and sooty, which crossed the destroyed tops of the Period V–VI walls. Not a single element of buildings in the royal quarter survived. The walls were ruthlessly rooted out, the stones perhaps to be re-used in houses on the lower slopes of the hill, where the immigrants settled by Sargon may have lived. The burnt debris of the actual destruction and the debris resulting from the robbing were then levelled over. In it were new pottery forms, probably to be associated with the immigrants, as well as Palestinian pottery of types later than that associated with the earlier periods,[16] with contacts with 7th century B.C. forms. The levelling-over process therefore took place sufficiently long after Sargon's conquest for pottery brought by the newcomers, and possibly by an Assyrian garrison, which it is to be presumed was present for some years, as well as the later Palestinian forms, to be lying about; a date early in the 7th century B.C. is probable. The structural evidence suggests that the newcomers were not allowed to settle

[11] SS 1, p. 103
[12] SS 1, pp. 106–8.
[13] SS 1, pp. 108–10.
[14] SS 1, pp. 106–8.
[15] SS 1, pp. 117–18.
[16] SS 3, pp. 125–9.

in the summit area, as they did at Megiddo. It must have been reserved for administrative purposes, though in the area excavated there was no evidence of buildings of the period.

No doubt all the towns that had remained to Israel after the earlier campaign were similarly destroyed, as the Biblical passage quoted above (p. 132) clearly suggests. Evidence of this has been recovered from Tirzah (T. el Far'ah), one of the nearest important towns to the south. As described above (p. 126), Tirzah had re-appeared as a town c. 800 B.C., contemporaneous with Samaria Period IV. This town was destroyed by fire,[17] and in the poor succeeding occupation the same types of imported pottery that are found at Samaria appeared. Shechem, the other important southern neighbour of Samaria, was likewise destroyed; the archaeological evidence shows a layer of burnt and collapsed debris nearly a metre thick,[18] and in the succeeding layer the same foreign pottery appears.[19] All the evidence is that the Israelite northern kingdom passes very literally out of existence, and the future of the area is that of a country occupied by a mixed people, regarded as racially impure by the strict Jews.

The Kingdom of Judah was more remote, and was sheltered from the first stages of the Assyrian advance by Israel, even though the two kingdoms seldom combined. The threat was, however, very near. King Ahaz in 733 B.C. had offered tribute to Tiglath-pileser[20] and he is mentioned among the vassal kings in one of Tiglath-pileser's lists.[21] Part of the duty of vassal kings was to recognise the state religion of the overlord.[22]

After Sargon had captured Samaria in 722–721 B.C., he advanced down the coast right up to the Egyptian border. The inhabitants of Judah in the hill country must have watched his progress with great trepidation.

As always, however, there was an ebb and flow in Assyrian advance, due to internal politics and the necessity facing each new king to establish himself. The real threat to Judah developed only under Sennacherib at the end of the 8th century B.C. In his campaign of 701 B.C., the great city of Lachish was destroyed, and his assault on the town is shown in reliefs found at Nineveh.[23] Other towns such as Beth-shemesh, Gibeah and T. Jemmeh, near Gaza, were also destroyed.[24]

Jerusalem was now the only Royal City left, and Jerusalem itself was besieged by the Assyrians. It was saved by a mixture of active defensive measures and diplomacy. The Biblical record appears most vividly in II Chronicles. Hezekiah, with perhaps a political reliance on Egypt against which the prophet Isaiah was continuously giving warning,[25] gives expression to his repudiation of allegiance to Assyria by eradicating

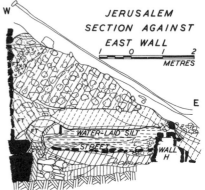

*Fig. 27. Section showing successive periods of later east wall at Jerusalem.*

[17] *R.B.* LVIII, pp. 417–20.
[18] G. E. Wright, *Shechem*, pp. 161–2.
[19] *Ibid.*, pp. 163–4.
[20] II Kings 16. 7–9.
[21] Gressmann, *Altorientalische Texte und Bilde zum Alten Testament*, p. 348.
[22] II Kings 16. 10–18; *Noth*, p. 266.
[23] In British Museum; see A. H. Layard, *Nineveh and Babylon*, p. 148.
[24] *A. in H.L.*, p. 286.
[25] Isaiah 30. 1–3; 31. 1–3.

*Pl. 93. The final eastern wall of the period of the monarchy at Jerusalem.*

foreign worship in Jerusalem, and in II Chronicles 29–31 we have his inspiring call to Judah and the remnants of Israel to unite in the pure worship of Yahweh. But II Chronicles 32 showed that Hezekiah also recognized that enthusiasm was not enough and that concrete defensive steps had to be taken. 'He set to work resolutely and built up all the wall that was broken down, and raised towers upon it, and outside it he built another wall.'[26] To the latter part of the existence of the kingdom of Judah belong several stages in the defences of Jerusalem. The evidence for the vanished wall that was the immediate successor of the Jebusite-Davidic town wall low on the eastern slope is described above (pp. 122–3). The levels associated with this wall are cut by a later wall, which itself has several building periods (fig. 27). The remains of this wall are impressive, and the views of it also indicate a succession of building periods (pl. 93). There is still much work to be done on the finds of the 1961–7 excavations to establish a close date

[26] II Chronicles 32.5.

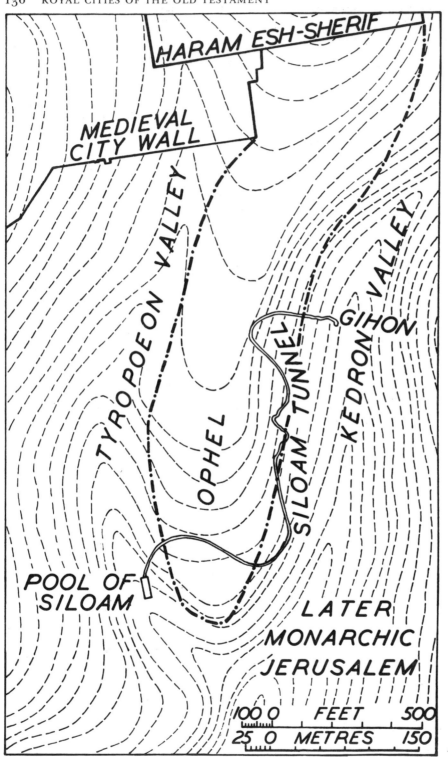

HARAM ESH-SHERIF

MEDIEVAL
CITY WALL

TYROPOEON VALLEY

OPHEL

SILOAM TUNNEL

GIHON

KEDRON VALLEY

POOL OF
SILOAM

LATER
MONARCHIC
JERUSALEM

100  0        FEET        500

25  0     METRES      150

*Fig. 28. Plan of Siloam tunnel.*

for these phases in the life of the final city wall of royal Jerusalem. We have no inscriptions or very closely datable finds, and a very exact pottery sequence will have to be established, firstly to compare finds from different excavation areas, and secondly to make comparisons with any other sites that offer useful dating evidence. From a preliminary assessment of the pottery evidence, it is very probable that one of the stages of this wall belongs to the time of Hezekiah, and was his response to the Assyrian threat, and it is very possible that he was responsible for the first build of this impressive wall unless the vanished wall (p. 123) is to be ascribed to him. This is therefore the first item of archaeological evidence for Hezekiah's defensive activities.

Hezekiah's attention to the town wall actually is given second place in the Biblical account. 'And when Hezekiah saw that Sennacherib had come and intended to fight against Jerusalem, he planned with his officers and his mighty men to stop the waters of the springs that were outside the city; and they helped him. A great many people were gathered, and they stopped all the springs and the brook that flowed through the land, saying, "Why should the kings of Assyria come and find much water?" '.[27] The Biblical reference is to springs in the plural. From the present evidence there is only one important spring, the Spring Gihon; lower in the Kedron valley was Bir Eyub, but this was somewhat south of the southern point of the city, and can never have had the same importance. We know nothing of any measures taken to conceal it, nor do we know of any other springs, other than winter torrents down the valleys, that can have been of significance.

The Spring Gihon must have been the principal object of Hezekiah's attention. Its importance in relation to the original site of Jerusalem has already been described (p. 23), and also the original water shaft giving access to it from within the city (pp. 25–26). At some stage within the earlier part of the period of the monarchy, the waters from the spring were apparently carried in a channel along the side of the ridge.[28] The final stage of the canalization of its waters was the famous Siloam tunnel (fig. 28), final since it still functions today. The first thorough exploration of the tunnel was that of Warren in 1867.[29] At that time, the rock-cut channel was silted almost to the roof, and the explorers had to wallow through on their stomachs, lighted by candles carried in their mouths, with all the attendant difficulties of making a plan in such circumstances. Shortly afterwards, in 1870, the dramatic discovery of the inscription on the rock-cut wall, recording the cutting of the tunnel, was accidentally made by a boy, the adopted son of the well-known American family, the Vesters, who founded

[27] II Chronicles 32. 2–4.
[28] Vincent, *J.s.T.*, pp. 6–8.
[29] Warren, *R.J.*, pp. 239–2.

Pl. 94. The Siloam tunnel at Jerusalem.          Pl. 95. The Siloam tunnel.

the American Colony.[30] The tunnel had been cut by two gangs, from the south and the north, and the inscription records the triumphant moment when they met: 'This is the story of the boring through: whilst [the tunnellers lifted] the pick each towards his fellows and whilst three cubits [yet remained] to be bored [through, there was heard] the voice of a man calling his fellow, for there was a split in the rock on the right hand and on [the left hand]. And on the day of the boring through, the tunnellers struck, each in the direction of his fellow, pick against pick. And the water started to flow from the source to the pool, twelve hundred cubits. A hundred cubits was the height of the rock above the level of the tunnellers.'

That they met at all was a remarkable feat. The planners had not even a magnetic compass to control their direction, still less elaborate instruments such as theodolites upon which a modern engineer would rely. The plan, fig. 95 does show a curiously winding course, which carried the water down the eastern flank of the hill and then ultimately across the tip of the hill into the central valley. Many suggestions have been made to account for the great and apparently unnecessary sweep before the final turn to the west. A favoured theory has been that it was to avoid the area in which were the royal tombs, the tombs of David and his successors, which were believed to have been discovered in the 1913–14 excavations.[31] Personally, I do not believe that the remains discovered were those of the royal tombs, nor that, so many metres below, the tunnel diggers would have realised, or even minded, that they were overhead. The simplest explanation is that the tunnel diggers went astray and did not follow the most direct line.

As we know the Siloam tunnel today, it is the result of the clearance of the silting, found by Warren, by the Parker expedition of 1911. This expedition never published its findings, but very fortunately Père Hugues Vincent, O.P., of the École Biblique, was allowed to visit and plan the tunnel with great exactness. Today one can still see the tunnel, and walk along it, in its original state as planned by Hezekiah (pls. 94 and 95).

The Siloam tunnel today ends in an open tank (pl. 98), which probably preserves traces of a rebuilding in Roman and Byzantine times. But it would be impossible to interpret the evidence in any other way than showing that the waters of Hezekiah's tunnel ran into a reservoir in the central valley. The evidence of the 1961–7 excavations is emphatic that the adjacent slopes of the western ridge were not within the contemporary city.[32] It would clearly have served Hezekiah very little to have carried the vital water supply from an exposed

[30] Bertha Vester, *Our Jerusalem*, pp. 95–97.
[31] Weill, *La Cité de David*.
[32] *P.E.Q.* 1962, pp. 84–86.

position on the eastern flank of the city to an only slightly less exposed place on the western flank. Strictly archaeological evidence does not provide the answer, but inference from existing remains can. Today, the overflow from the present pool runs down a channel beneath the tip of the rock base of the eastern ridge (pl. 96). The present channel is at the foot of a scarping of the rock that has clearly removed its outer wall (pl. 97). It can be taken as certain that originally the overflow ran out into the Kedron valley to the east in a rock-cut channel, of which the mouth could have been so disguised or the water so diffused that an enemy would have had little guidance as to the source of the water. This implies emphatically that the reservoir for the water in the central valley was as concealed as was its overflow, which basically would have run much more simply down the centre of the valley. The answer to the problem is therefore ·that Hezekiah's tunnel conducted the water from the Spring Gihon to a rock-cut cistern, presumably of a very considerable size, in the central valley, from which a rock-cut channel carried the overflow down into the Kedron. This concealed cistern could have had access from within the town by stairs or a shaft, on familiar Palestinian patterns. The collapse of the roof of this ambitious cistern, and of any systems of access, would have created the surroundings of the present Pool, and this solution could be supported by the existence of a concavity in the present contours to the east.

*Pl. 96. View of scarp that truncated the south end of the ridge on which the original city was situated.*

Pl. 97. Outflow channel from Pool of Siloam, with outer wall removed by scarping.

Pl. 98. The Pool of Siloam today.

*Pl. 99. Houses of the 7th century B.C. at Jerusalem built on the stone filling of the Jebusite terraces.*

There is thus supporting archaeological evidence for the Biblical record of some of Hezekiah's measures to defend Jerusalem against the Assyrians. Archaeology does not, of course, provide evidence of Hezekiah's attempt to buy off Sennacherib,[33] nor of the plague which the Biblical record suggests was the ultimate cause of the Assyrian withdrawal.[34] But it is on all counts clear that the kingdom of Judah and Jerusalem survived the Assyrian threat for a hundred years, though the independence of Judah was very nominal.

Almost the only buildings of the period of the monarchy to survive in Jerusalem that have been found belong to this last century of its existence. They have been uncovered at the crest of the steep slope on the eastern side of the eastern ridge. They are founded almost directly on the Jebusite terrace structure (pl. 99) which from the thirteenth century or so onwards had converted this slope into a reasonably convenient building area. All the houses that through the intervening six centuries or so had stood on these terraces had in turn collapsed and for the most part have completely disappeared. The reason for this is simple. The whole terrace structure was dependent on the retaining walls that supported it. Every break in a retaining wall had, in view of the steepness of the slope, a disastrous effect on the houses that stood on the terrace above. Within a short time, with great probability at least by the time of the next winter's rains, they would crumble down the slope below. The evidence is quite conclusive, in that the underlying terraces belong to the Late Bronze Age, and the only surviving houses based thereon belong to the 7th century B.C.

The houses are not impressive (pl. 100). The rooms are for the most part small. The masonry is rough. The floors are of mud plaster. The original appearance of the walls would certainly not have been quite so unattractive, for the roughly dressed and coursed stones would have been covered by a mud plaster, some traces of which can still be seen. The small area that survived the subsequent destruction was clearly built in a series of terraces, and a staircase between two of them, actually a secondary structure, is visible in pl. 100. Though the plan was incomplete, owing to the subsequent destruction, it is clear that in the area uncovered there was only one room of any size. This was of a tripartite plan, standard in the Palestinian Iron Age II, in which a central nave is divided from two side aisles by two rows of monolithic piers. Two piers in one of these rows were uncovered (pl. 103). The easternmost line of piers has disappeared in the final destruction to be described below.

The houses are to be interpreted as ordinary domestic structures. There is nothing in their plan or construction that

*Pl. 99. Houses of the 7th century B.C. at Jerusalem built on the stone filling of the Jebusite terraces.*

[33] II Kings 18. 14–16.
[34] II Chronicles 32. 21.

Pl. 100. General view of the houses of the 7th century B.C. from north.

Pl. 101. Oven in houses of 7th century B.C.

demands any other interpretation. In one room was an ordinary domestic oven (pl. 101). The most interesting find was that in the ruins of one room were thirty-four weights, dome-shaped objects in polished limestone, many of them marked with their weights in shekels, n-s-p. or p-y-m., ranging in weight from a quarter n-s-p. (2·57 gm) to 24 shekels (268·24 gm.). There could be a suggestion of an official use of this house, but an interpretation of the house as a shop of a merchant or craftsman is more probable.

In general, it can be concluded that these structures show a typical section of the domestic quarter of Jerusalem in the period of the monarchy. Similar buildings are found in all the contemporary towns and villages of Judah that have been excavated. The native architecture of the period was undistinguished. To the north were the Temple and royal palaces, and probably official buildings as well, but of these no remnants survive. Probably the architecture was more pretentious, but we cannot tell to what extent the fine Phoenician masonry of Solomon's period survived intervening destructions. If the evidence from Megiddo is any guide, the elegance of much of the original buildings may have been lost with the re-use of the fine individual blocks and architectural features in positions for which they were not designed.

During the 7th century B.C., the situation of the Kingdom of Judah was precarious. Towards the end of the century, there was a revival under King Josiah, due to the decline of Assyria in its homeland. Josiah not only abolished the worship of Assyrian gods enforced by the dominant Assyrians,[35] but gradually brought districts of the old kingdom of Israel under his rule; the evidence of this is given by the lists of towns included in his administrative districts.[36] This brief revival came to an end when the Egyptians under Necho tried to take advantage of the weakness of Assyria and re-establish their rule in Palestine and Syria. Josiah was killed by Necho at Megiddo in 609 B.C. But Egyptian interference was in itself short-lived. The Medes and Babylonians broke up the remnants of the Assyrian Empire and the Babylonians established themselves in the southern part of Mesopotamia. By 604 B.C. the Babylonians, under the leadership of Nebuchadnezzar (more correctly Nebuchadrezzar), had defeated Necho and resumed possession of Syria and Palestine.

Jehoiakim of Judah was apparently not convinced of the power of the new rulers, and revolted, probably twice, in 602 B.C. and 598 B.C. The Babylonian capture of Jerusalem in the latter year and the renewed subjugation of Judah was the beginning of the end for Jerusalem as a Royal City. Jerusalem fell after a siege, and Jehoiachin, son of Jehoiakim, was carried

[35] II Kings 23. 4.
[36] Cf. *Noth*, pp. 273–4.

away into captivity in Babylon, with 'all Jerusalem, and all the princes, and all the mighty men of valour, ten thousand captives, and all the craftsmen and the smiths; none remained, except the poorest people of the land'.[37] The material damage to Jerusalem was apparently confined to sacking the Temple and Palace. Nebuchadnezzar 'carried off all the treasures of the house of the Lord, and the treasures of the king's house and cut in pieces all the vessels of gold in the temple of the Lord, which Solomon king of Israel had made, as the Lord had foretold'.[38]

In Jehoiachin's place Nebuchadnezzar established Jehoiachin's uncle Zedekiah as king, probably ruling over a kingdom of reduced size, with the southern part handed over to the Edomites.[39] The unrest in Jerusalem and the mutterings of the inhabitants against the Bablyonian rule may be judged from the Book of Jeremiah.[40] Jeremiah was convinced that, because of the evil-doings of the people of Judah, the Lord had placed them under the rule of the king of Babylon. 'For thus says the Lord of hosts, the God of Israel: I have put upon the neck of all these nations an iron yoke of servitude to Nebuchadnezzar king of Babylon, and they shall serve him, for I had given him even the beasts of the field.'[41] It is not hard to imagine the unpopularity of such advice, and eventually Zedekiah was persuaded to ignore it and to revolt. 'And Zedekiah rebelled against the king of Babylon. And in the ninth year of his reign, in the tenth month, on the tenth day of the month, Nebuchadnezzar king of Babylon came with all his army against Jerusalem, and laid siege to it; and they built siegeworks against it round about: so the city was besieged till the eleventh year of King Zedekiah.'[42]

It is probable that Zedekiah was tempted to revolt by the hope of help from Egypt, for the Egyptian king was no more reconciled to Babylonian rule in Egypt's old provinces of Palestine and Syria than were the inhabitants. Certainly while the Babylonian army was ravaging Judah, Zedekiah sent an emissary to Egypt, and we can suppose that this was to ask for Egyptian intervention, though the significance of the record is not clear. Evidence of this comes from the Lachish Letters,[43] a group of documents written on potsherds found in the ruins of the gatehouse of Lachish, one of the major cities of southwest Judah. One letter shows how, while Jerusalem was being besieged, the rest of the kingdom was being overrun. The writer of the document was apparently in a place between Jerusalem and Lachish, and was accustomed to receive signals from Lachish via the intermediate post of Azeqah. But Azeqah must have fallen, for the letter says 'for the signal-stations of Lachish we are watching, according to all the signs that my

[37] II Kings, 24. 14.
[38] II Kings 24. 13.
[39] *Noth*, p. 283.
[40] Jeremiah 27–29.
[41] Jeremiah 28. 14.
[42] II Kings 24. 20 to 25. 2.
[43] *L I.*

lord gives, because we do not see [the signals of] Azeqah'.[44] Lachish must have been the last place to fall except Jerusalem, for when during the siege Jeremiah once more warned Zedekiah of the impending fall of Jerusalem, the situation is thus described: 'When the army of the king of Babylon was fighting against Jerusalem and against all the cities of Judah that were left, Lachish and Azeqah; for these were the only fortified cities of Judah that remained'.[45]

It was during this last desperate stage that Zedekiah sent his emissary to Egypt. 'Down went the commander of the army [Yi]khbaryahu the son of Elnatan to come to Egypt.'[46] Certainly there was an Egyptian expedition into Judah during the siege. 'The army of Pharaoh had come out of Egypt; and when the Chaldeans who were besieging Jerusalem heard news of them, they withdrew from Jerusalem.'[47]

The respite was only temporary, but it must have been a great help in prolonging the stand of the city, for it would have enabled it to be re-victualled, always providing that the whole land had not been so ravaged that no food supplies were available. It would seem in fact that it was famine which caused the ultimate collapse, after the siege had lasted (presumably with this interval of withdrawal) for a period of eighteen months, from the tenth day of the tenth month of the ninth year of Zedekiah's reign to the ninth day of the fourth month of his eleventh year. This is a great tribute to the strength of the defences. At least one part of the wall that withstood the Babylonian attack can be identified, the final stage of the wall exposed on the eastern slope (pl. 93). The great strength of this wall lay in the fact that outside it the slope drops very rapidly, which would hamper the attackers' freedom of manœuvre and the use of battering rams, while it was built against steeply rising rock on its inner side, which would strengthen it appreciably if battering rams were used. From its summit, the defences could easily dominate attackers on the slopes below with even the simple projectiles that were probably available, sling-stones and arrows. On the west side, the wall has not been found, but it is clear that it must have run along the crest of the slope of the central valley, with a similarly dominating position. Only to the north was there no physical feature to give strength, but this must have been provided by the great podium of the Temple. It must also be taken that an additional source of strength was an assured water-supply, and that Hezekiah's diversion of the water of the Spring Gihon into a hidden cistern in the central valley was still functioning (see pp. 137–40).

Eventually resistance collapsed. 'On the ninth day of the fourth month the famine was sore in the city, so that there was

[44] *L I*, pp. 79–87.
[45] Jeremiah 34. 7.
[46] *L I*, p. 51.
[47] Jeremiah 37. 5.

no bread for the people of the land. Then a breach was made in the city, and all the men of war fled by night . . . (now the Chaldeans were against the city round about).'[48] Their flight was down the Kedron valley towards the Jordan, but they were overtaken in the plains of Jericho. The army was scattered. Zedekiah was taken prisoner, blinded and sent in captivity to Babylon. Thus ended in the year 587 B.C., the kingship founded by David.

Jerusalem was savagely sacked: 'Now in the fifth month, on the seventh day of the month, which was the nineteenth year of King Nebuchadnezzar, king of Babylon, came Nebuzaradan, the captain of the guard, a servant of the king of Babylon, unto Jerusalem: and he burnt the house of the Lord, and the King's house; and all the houses of Jerusalem, even every great house burnt he with fire. And all the army of the Chaldeans who were with the captain of the guard, brake down the walls of Jerusalem round about.'[49] The inhabitants were all carried into exile except 'of the poorest in the land to be vinedressers and ploughmen.'[50] The Temple had been partially sacked in 598 B.C., but this time all the ancient treasures and fitments were plundered. The description of what was removed[51] is the counterpart of the description of the furnishing of the Temple by Solomon.[52] Probably the Ark of the Covenant vanished in the burning of the Temple, though there is no actual reference to it subsequent to its deposit in the Holy of Holies in the time of Solomon.

From the limited area in which archaeological evidence of this period survives, a vivid picture can be deduced of the effect of this destruction. The most disastrous element was undoubtedly the breaking down of 'the walls around Jerusalem'. The burning of the Temple, palace and great houses would have left them as roofless ruins with calcined walls. But many of them could have been repairable. The vulnerable parts of the city were those that stood on the slopes, of which the very foundations were dependent on the walls that supported the terraces. The whole of the eastern half of the original city was thus dependent; elsewhere, breaches in the defences along the crest may have endangered the houses in the immediate vicinity, but the effect would not have been far-reaching. On the eastern slope, the system of terraces that provided building space has been described (pp. 33–35). Each of these was buttressed by lower elements in the system, and the ultimate support was the town wall at the base. Each breach in this wall would have a cumulative undermining effect on the structures higher up the hill. The effect of winter rains in Jerusalem today is shown in pl. 102. The spread uphill of terrace collapses is shown on pl. 103. This shows the room described above (p.

[48] II Kings 25. 3–4.
[49] II Kings 25. 8–10.
[50] II Kings 25. 12.
[51] II Kings 25. 13–17.
[52] I Kings 7. 15–50.

Pl. 102. Recent rainwater gullies illustrating erosion on the eastern slopes of ancient Jerusalem.

Pl. 103. Stone tumble associated with the final destruction of monarchic Jerusalem in 587 B.C.

143) as the largest of the 7th century B.C. rooms exposed. The easternmost of the two lines of monoliths that certainly existed has disappeared with the collapse of the adjacent retaining wall. Crossing the broken edge of the floor are tip-lines of wash disappearing down the hill at an angle of 40°. On the floor of the room, enveloping the two surviving monolithic piers, is an enormous collapse of building stones from the superstructure of the house. Part of this collapse, and that of terraces and the buildings that they supported lower down the slope, descends right down the slope in a complete cascade of stones, and in this stone tumble the whole eastern section of Jerusalem disappeared.

When Cyrus the Great, now master of Babylon, allowed some of the exiles to return to Jerusalem, in 530 B.C., they must have patched up the better preserved houses on the summit of the ridge, and by 516 B.C. the Temple had been rebuilt. But there was no rebuilding of the king's palace, and Jerusalem was no longer a Royal City. It was many years before it was even a walled city again. When at last, probably c. 440 B.C., Nehemiah was allowed to rebuild the walls, he found the eastern side still abandoned and in such a chaos of tumbled stones that the Kedron valley was virtually impassable. His rebuilding was confined to the summit ridge, in places only 100 m. in width, and only a mutilated fragment of ancient Jerusalem remained to form the basis of the post-Exilic city.

# BIBLIOGRAPHY

ABBREVIATIONS

| | Amiran, R. Philistine Civilisation in the Light of Finds in Palestine and Egypt. *Eretz Israel* V (Hebrew with English summary). |
|---|---|
| *A. in H.L.* | *Archaeology in the Holy Land.* K. M. Kenyon, London, Ernest Benn. 1960. |
| *Amorites and Canaanites* | *Amorites and Canaanites.* Schweich Lectures. K. M. Kenyon. Oxford University Press for the British Academy. 1966. |
| | *Arslan Tash.* F. Thureau-Dangin, A. Barrois, G. Dossin and M. Dunand. Paris, Bibliothèque archéologique et historique, Vol. XVI. 1931. |
| *B. and D.* | *Excavations at Jerusalem 1894–1897.* F. J. Bliss and A. C. Dickie. London, Palestine Exploration Fund, 1898. |
| *Barnett, Nimrud Ivories* | *Catalogue of the Nimrud Ivories with Other Examples of Ancient Near Eastern Ivories in the British Museum.* London. 1957. |
| *Beth-shan. Four Temples* | *The Four Canaanite Temples of Beth-shan.* Beth-shan Reports, Vol. II, Pt. 1. A. Rowe. University of Pennsylvania. 1940. |
| | *The Iron Age at Beth-shan.* F. W. James. Museum Monographs. University of Pennsylvania. 1966. |
| *C.A.H.* | *Cambridge Ancient History.* Revised edition. References are to fascicles of the interim publication. |
| *Gezer, I, II, III* | *The Excavations of Gezer 1902–1905 and 1907–1909.* R. A. Stewart Macalister. London, Palestine Exploration Fund. 1912. |
| *H I* | *Hazor I.* Y. Yadin, Y. Aharoni, R. Amiran, T. Dothan, I. Dunayevski, J. Perrot. Hebrew University, Jerusalem. 1958. |
| *H II* | *Hazor II.* Y. Yadin, Y. Aharoni, R. Amiran, T. Dothan, I. Dunayevski, J. Perrot. Hebrew University, Jerusalem. 1960. |
| *H III–IV* | *Hazor III–IV.* Y. Yadin, Y. Aharoni, R. Amiran, T. Dothan, I. Dunayevski, J. Perrot. Hebrew University, Jerusalem. 1961 (plates only). |
| *Jericho I, II* | *Excavations at Jericho.* K. M. Kenyon. British School of Archaeology in Jerusalem, London. 1960 and 1965. |
| *Joseph to Joshua* | *From Joseph to Joshua.* Schweich Lectures. H. H. Rowley. Oxford University Press for the British Academy. 1950. |
| | Kenyon, K. M. Megiddo, Hazor, Samaria and Chronology. *University of London Institute of Archaeology Bulletin 4.* 1964. |
| *L I* | *Lachish I. The Lachish Letters.* H. Torczyner, L. Harding, A. Lewis, J. L. Starkey. Oxford University Press. 1938. |
| *L III* | *Lachish III. The Iron Age.* O. Tufnell. Oxford University Press. 1953. |
| *Macalister* | *Excavations on the Hill of Ophel, Jerusalem 1923–1925.* R. A. S. Macalister and J. G. Duncan. London. Annual of the Palestine Exploration Fund IV. 1926. |
| *M I* | *Megiddo I. Seasons of 1925–34, Strata I–V.* R. S. Lamon and |

|  |  |
|---|---|
| | G. M. Shipton. Oriental Institute Publications XLII. University of Chicago. 1948. |
| *M II* | *Megiddo II. Seasons of 1935–39.* G. Loud. Oriental Institute Publications LXII. University of Chicago. 1948. |
| | *The Megiddo Water System.* R. S. Lamon. Oriental Institute Publications XXXII. University of Chicago. 1935. |
| | *The Megiddo Ivories.* G. Loud. Oriental Institute Publications LII. University of Chicago. 1939. |
| | *Material Remains of the Megiddo Cult.* H. G. May. Oriental Institute Publications XXVI. University of Chicago. 1935. |
| *Nimrud* | *Nimrud and its Remains.* M. E. L. Mallowan. London. Collins. 1966. |
| *Noth* | *The History of Israel.* M. Noth. London, A. & C. Black. Second English edition. 1959. |
| | Pendlebury, W. The Relationship between Philistine and Mycenaean Pottery. *Q.D.A.P.* V. 3. |
| | Petrie, W. M. F. *Tell el Hesy (Lachish).* London. 1891. |
| *Samaria H.E.* | *Harvard Excavations at Samaria 1908–1910.* G. A Reisner, C. S. Fisher, D. G. Lyon. Harvard University Press. 1924. |
| *SS 1* | *Samaria-Sebaste 1. The Buildings of Samaria.* J. W. Crowfoot, K. M. Kenyon, E. L. Sukenik. London, Palestine Exploration Fund. 1942. |
| *SS 2* | *Samaria-Sebaste 2. Early Ivories from Samaria.* J. W. Crowfoot, G. M. Crowfoot. London, Palestine Exploration Fund. 1938. |
| | *Samaria-Sebaste 3. The Objects from Samaria.* J. W. Crowfoot, G. M. Crowfoot, K. M. Kenyon. London, Palestine Exploration Fund. 1957. |
| *Sendschirli IV* | *Ausgrabungen in Sendschirli IV.* F. von Luschan *et al.* Berlin. 1911. |
| *Simons* | *Jerusalem in the Old Testament.* J. Simons, S. J. Leiden, E. J. Brill. 1952. |
| | Vester, B. S. *Our Jerusalem.* Published by the author, Lebanon. 1950. |
| *Vincent, J. de l'A. T.* | *Jerusalem de l'Ancien Testament.* L. H. Vincent, O.P., A. M. Steve, O.P. Paris, J. Gabalda et Cie. 1954 and 1956. |
| *Vincent, J.s.T.* | *Jerusalem sous Terre. Les récentes Fouilles d'Ophel.* H. V(incent). London, Horace Cox. 1911. |
| *Warren 1867–70* | *Excavations at Jerusalem 1867–70.* Captain Charles Warren. London, Palestine Exploration Fund. 1884. |
| *Warren, U.J.* | *Underground Jerusalem.* Captain Charles Warren. |
| *Warren, R.J.* | *The Recovery of Jerusalem.* Captain Charles Warren. |
| *Weill* | *La Cité de David.* R. Weill. Paris. 1920 and 1947. |
| | Wright, G. E. *Shechem.* New York, McGraw-Hill. 1965. |
| | Yadin, Y. Ancient Judean Weights and the Date of the Samaria Ostraea. *Scripta Hierosolymitana* VIII. Hebrew University. |

JOURNAL
ABBREVIATIONS

| | |
|---|---|
| *A.A.S.O.R.* | Annual of the American Schools of Oriental Research. New Haven, Conn. |
| *B.A.* | *The Biblical Archaeologist.* American Schools of Oriental Research. Cambridge, Mass. |
| *Eretz Israel* | Annual of the Israel Exploration Society. Jerusalem, Israel. |
| *I.E.J.* | *Israel Exploration Journal.* Jerusalem, Israel. |
| *P.E.Q.* | *Palestine Exploration Quarterly.* Palestine Exploration Fund. |
| *Q.D.A.P.* | *Quarterly of the Department of Antiquities of Palestine.* Oxford University Press. |
| *R.B.* | *Revue Biblique.* École Biblique et Archéologique de St. Étienne, Jerusalem. |

# ACKNOWLEDGEMENTS

# Acknowledgements and References to Illustrations

The photographs of Jerusalem are the copyright of the Jerusalem Excavation Fund, and are the work of the expedition's photographers, Miss N. Lord, Miss C. Western and P. G. Dorrell. Plans of Jerusalem are the work of the expedition's surveyors and draftsmen, Père Rousée, W. Ball, B. Johnson, P. Pilkington and T. Holland. T. Holland also did a number of the other drawings.

Thanks for permission to reproduce are due to:

Elia, Photographer, Jerusalem, pl. 2.

Schweig, pl. 3.

Professor Sir Max Mallowan, pls. 23, 24, 56, 57, 58, 59, 60, 61, 62.

Trustees of the British Museum, pl. 25.

Oriental Institute of Chicago, pls. 26, 30, 31, 32, 33, 34, 35, 64, 65, 66, 67, 68, 69, 70; figs. 12, 20, 21, 22, 26.

Professor Y. Yadin and the James A. de Rothschild Expedition at Hazor, pls. 28, 29, 71, 72; figs. 24, 25.

Professor Y. Yadin, figs. 10, 11, 15.

Palestine Exploration Fund, pls. 37, 41, 42, 43, 44, 45, 46, 47, 48, 49, 50, 51, 63, 92; figs. 16, 17, 18, 19.

Royal Air Force, pls. 39 and 40.

Librairie Orientaliste Paul Geuthner, Paris, pls. 52, 53, 54, 55.

D. Ussiskin, fig. 13.

Clarendon Press, fig. 2.

*References to Sources of Illustrations*

Pl. 23. *Nimrud II*, no. 482.
Pl. 24. *Nimrud II*, no. 501.
Pl. 26. *Material Remains of the Megiddo Cult*, pl. XVIII.
Pl. 28. *Hazor I*, pl. I.
Pl. 29. *Hazor III–IV*, pl. III.
Pl. 30. *Megiddo II*, fig. 108.
Pl. 31. *Megiddo II*, fig. 111.
Pl. 32. *Megiddo II*, fig. 95.
Pl. 33. *Megiddo I*, fig. 21.
Pl. 34. *Megiddo I*, fig. 15.
Pl. 35. *Megiddo I*, fig. 13.
Pl. 37. *Gezer I*, fig. 115.
Pl. 42. *SS I*, pl. XIV, 1.
Pl. 43. *SS I*, pl. XV, 2.
Pl. 44. *SS I*, pl. XXXI, 1.
Pl. 45. *SS I*, pl. XXIV, 2.
Pl. 46. *SS 2*, pl. I, 1.
Pl. 47. *SS 2*, pl. II, 1.
Pl. 48. *SS 2*, pl. V, 1.
Pl. 49. *SS 2*, pl. IX, 1.
Pl. 50. *SS 2*, pl. XX, 1.
Pl. 51. *SS 2*, pl. XVI, 2.
Pl. 52. *Arslan Tash*, pl. XIX, 2.
Pl. 53. *Arslan Tash*, pl. XLIV, 94.
Pl. 54. *Arslan Tash*, pl. XLVI, 105.
Pl. 55. *Arslan Tash*, pl. XXXI, 31.
Pl. 56. *Nimrud II*, no. 385.
Pl. 57. *Nimrud II*, no. 391.
Pl. 58. *Nimrud II*, no. 528.
Pl. 59. *Nimrud II*, no. 511.
Pl. 60. *Nimrud II*, no. 581A.
Pl. 61. *Nimrud II*, no. 541A.
Pl. 63. *SS I*, pl. XIII, 2.
Pl. 64. *Megiddo I*, fig. 60.
Pl. 65. *Megiddo I*, fig. 51.
Pl. 67. *Megiddo I*, fig. 44.
Pl. 68. *Megiddo I*, fig. 41.
Pl. 69. *Megiddo Water System*, fig. 12.
Pl. 70. *Megiddo Water System*, fig. 14.
Pl. 71. *Hazor III–IV*, pl. XXXII, 1.
Pl. 72. *Hazor II*, pl. IV, 2.
Pl. 92. *SS I*, pl. XX, 1.

Fig. 2. After *Oxford Bible Atlas*, H. G. May, p. 69.
Fig. 3. After Bliss and Dickie (folder).
Fig. 10. *I.E.J.* 8, p. 84, fig. 2.
Fig. 11. *I.E.J.* 8, p. 85, fig. 4.
Fig. 12. *Megiddo I*, fig. 12.
Fig. 13. *I.E.J.* 16, p. 182, fig. 4.
Fig. 15. *I.E.J.* 8, p. 84, fig. 3.
Fig. 16. *SS I*, pl. VII, A–B.
Fig. 17. *SS I*, pl. II.
Fig. 18. *SS I*, pl. VII, E–F.
Fig. 19. *SS I*, fig. 48.
Fig. 20. *Megiddo I*, fig. 3.
Fig. 21. *Megiddo I*, fig. 49.
Fig. 22. *Megiddo I*, fig. 34.
Fig. 24. *Hazor II*, pl. CXCVIII.
Fig. 25. *Hazor II*, pl. CCV.
Fig. 26. *Megiddo I*, fig. 72.

# INDEX